Reading First 2

Abe Dulay Wone

WorldCom Edu

How to **Read** **Reading First**

Illustration / Photo

Illustrations (for fictional and nonfiction passages) and photographs (for nonfiction passages) designed to introduce keywords and help predict the story before reading

Get Ready

Pre-reading questions designed to help students broaden their background knowledge and increase their interest in the topic of the unit

Key Words

Pre-reading vocabulary activities with photographs designed to practice key words in the story

Passage

Informative and high-interest fiction / nonfiction story that develops students' reading skills and expands knowledge in school subject areas

Look

One simple question or statement designed to build up more interest in reading

Check!

One sentence statements to check accuracy and speed in reading the passage

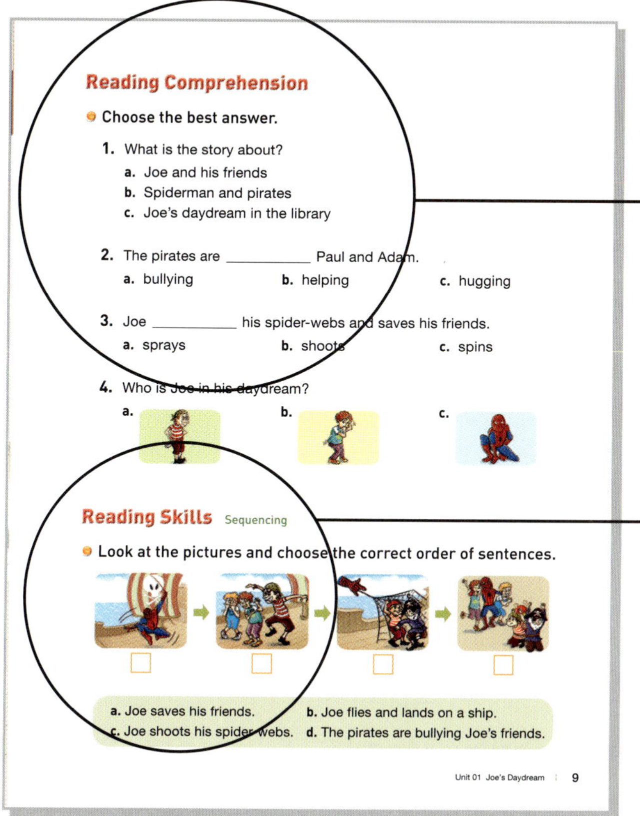

Reading Comprehension

Comprehension questions designed to test students' understanding of the passage and develop key reading skills such as the main idea and details

Reading Skills

Presents graphic organizers designed to help students grasp an idea of the unit

Word Challenge

- Variations in vocabulary activities to reinforce the key words from the unit
- Listening exercises to improve students' ability to understand words

Your Turn

Questions related to the reading content that can be used for extended speaking and writing practice and offer in-depth studies of the unit

Contents

Chapter 1

01 JOE's DAYDREAM

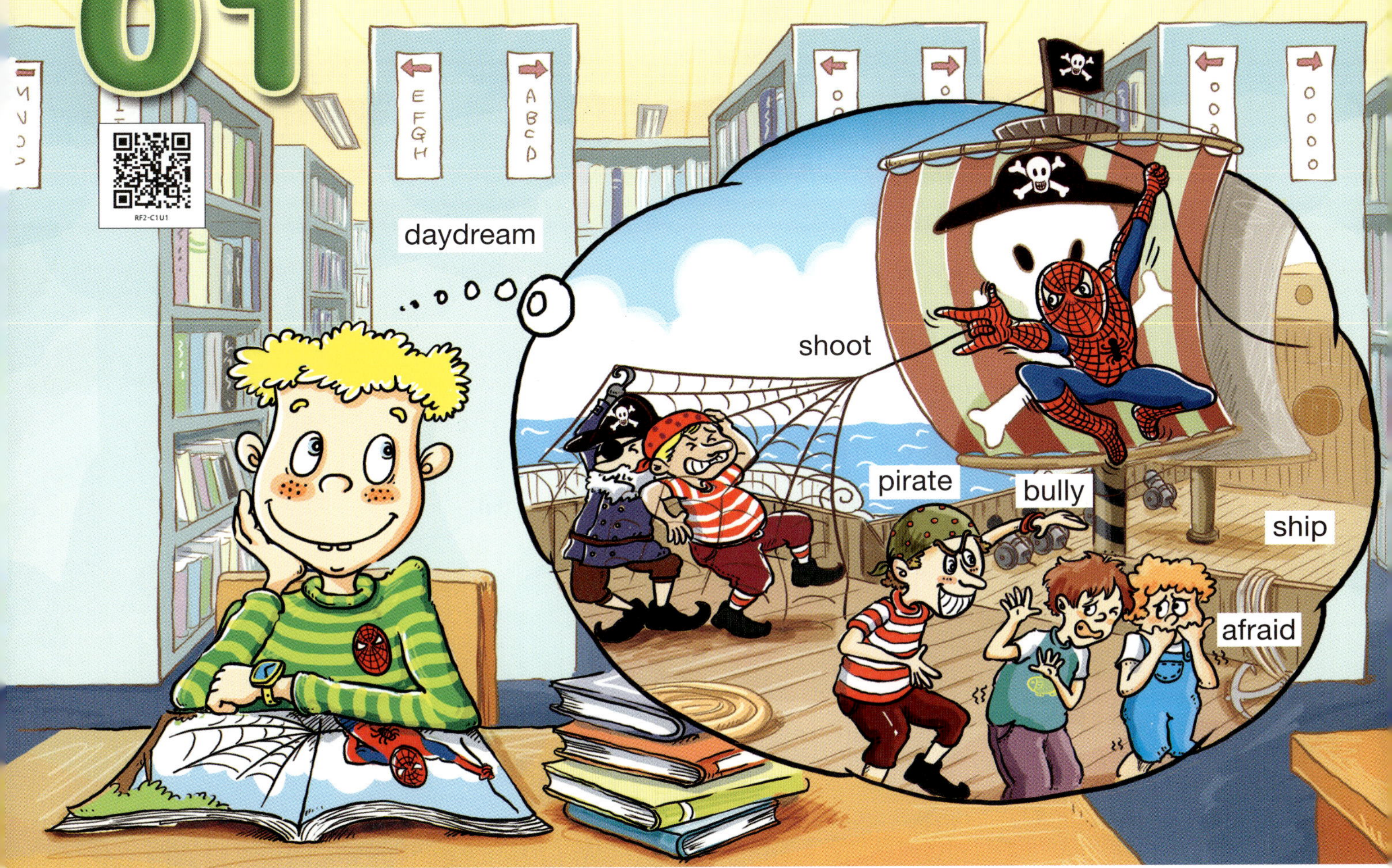

Get Ready

Look at the picture and talk about it.

1. Where is the boy?
2. What is the boy doing?

Key Words

- Listen and write. MP3 02

1 ____________

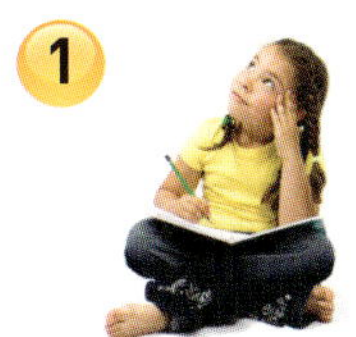

2 ____________

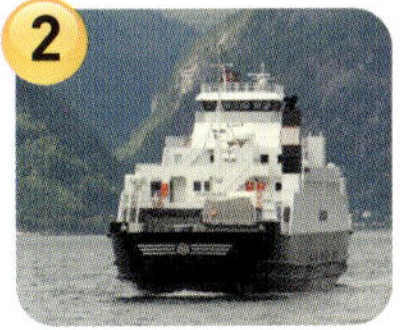

3 ____________

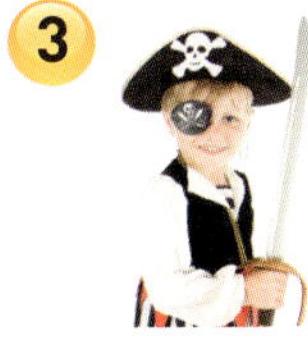

4 ____________

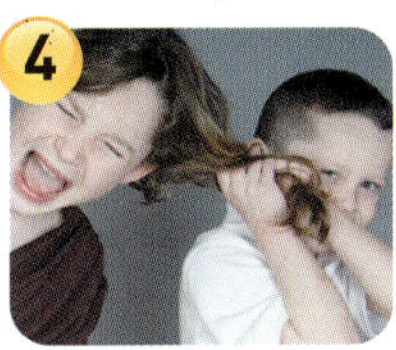

5 ____________

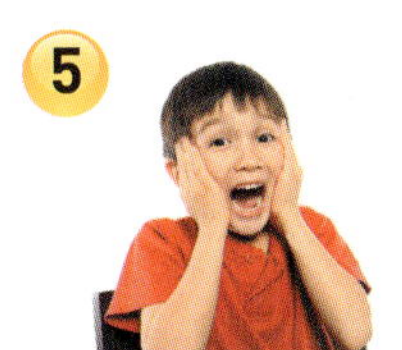

6 ____________

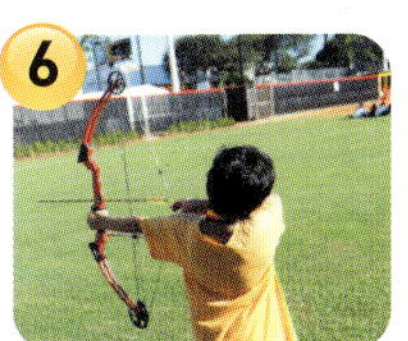

Joe is in the library.

He reads a book about Spiderman.

He starts daydreaming.

In his daydream , Joe is Spiderman.

He flies up to the sky.

He lands on a ship .

Joe sees his friends, Paul and Adam.

The pirates are bullying them.

They are afraid of the pirates.

Joe shoots his spider-webs. Twang! Twang!

The pirates fall one after another.

Joe saves his friends.

Look!

- How many pirates are on the ship?
- → There are ________ pirates.

Check!

	True	False
1. Joe is in his room.	☐	☐
2. Joe reads a book about Batman.	☐	☐
3. Joe is a pirate in his daydream.	☐	☐

Reading Comprehension

● **Choose the best answer.**

1. What is the story about?

    a. Joe and his friends

    b. Spiderman and pirates

    c. Joe's daydream in the library

2. The pirates are ______________ Paul and Adam.

    a. bullying   **b.** helping   **c.** hugging

3. Joe ______________ his spider-webs and saves his friends.

    a. sprays   **b.** shoots   **c.** spins

4. Who is Joe in his daydream?

    a.    **b.**    **c.** 

Reading Skills   Sequencing

● **Look at the pictures and choose the correct order of sentences.**

a. Joe saves his friends.   **b.** Joe flies and lands on a ship.

c. Joe shoots his spider-webs.   **d.** The pirates are bullying Joe's friends.

Word Challenge

- **Complete the word.**

1. ☐☐ip

2. pi☐☐te

3. sh☐☐t

- **Listen and write the correct word.** MP3 06

   4. We are _______________ of snakes.

   5. In her _______________, she is a princess.

   6. He likes to _______________ his little brother.

Your Turn

- **Look at the pictures. Then talk about what Suzy is daydreaming about.**

02 True Friend?

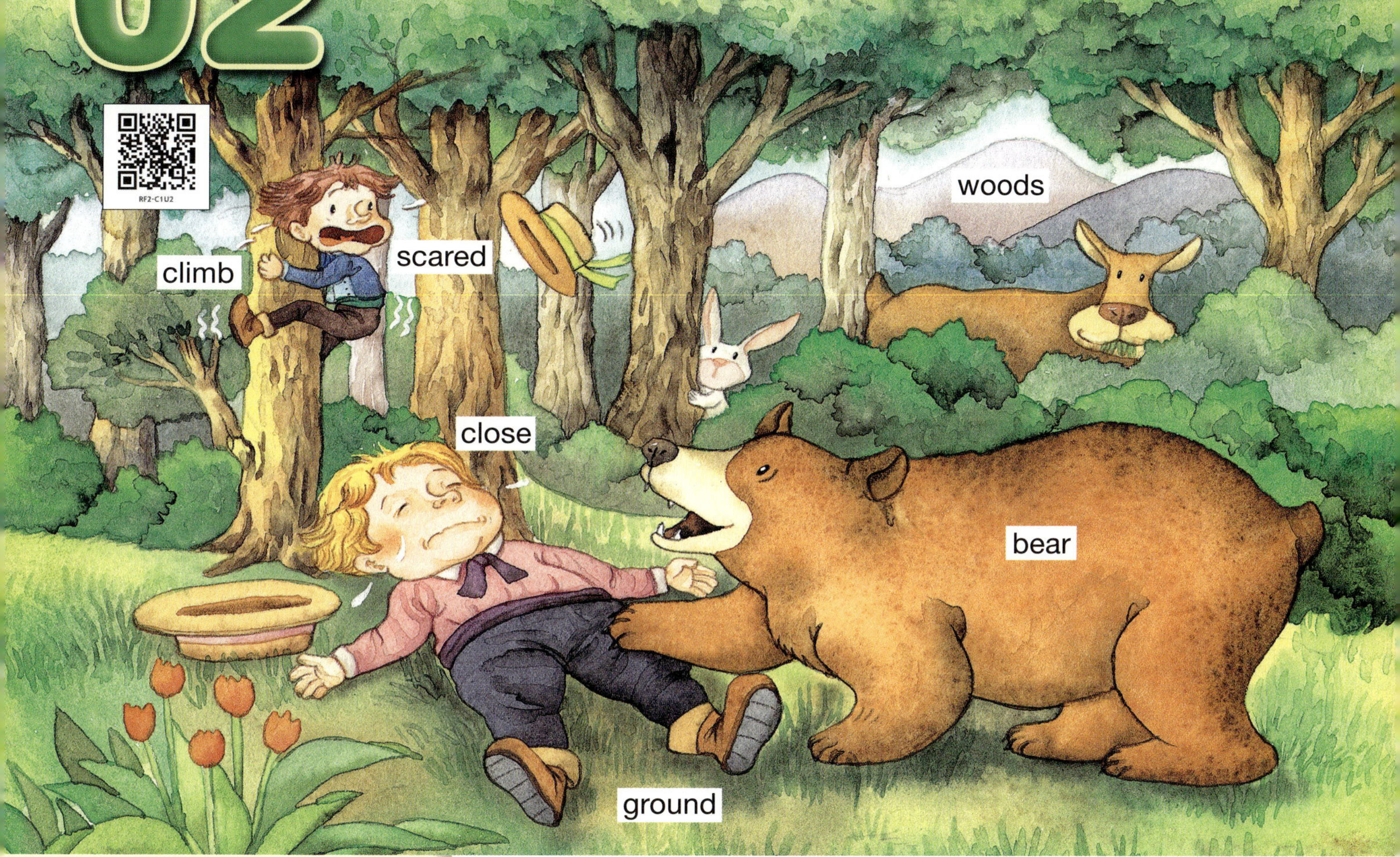

Get Ready

Look at the picture and talk about it.

1. What do you see in the picture?
2. What are the two boys doing?

Key Words

🟠 **Listen and write.** 🎵 07

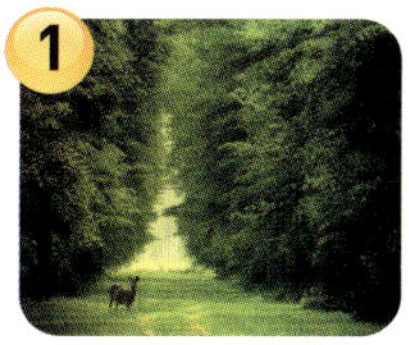

____

____

Look!

- Who is Tom in the picture? Circle him.

Check!

	True	False
1. Mike and Tom are in the woods.	☐	☐
2. Tom hides behind the bush.	☐	☐
3. Mike is Tom's true friend.	☐	☐

Reading Comprehension

● **Choose the best answer.**

1. What is the story about?

    a. a bear in the woods **b.** walking in the woods **c.** making a true friend

2. Tom is ___________ and closes his eyes.

    a. sad   **b.** scared   **c.** tired

3. What lesson did the bear give to Tom?

    a. Don't come to the woods.
    b. Choose your friend carefully.
    c. Learn how to climb a mountain.

4. What shows up in the woods?

a.    **b.**    **c.** 

Reading Skills Story Map

● **Fill in the chart.**

Place	Characters
In the ___________	Mike, Tom and a ___________

Beginning	Suddenly, a bear shows up.
Middle	Mike ___________ up a tree and Tom ___________ on the ground.
Ending	The bear says to Tom " ___________ your friend carefully!"

Word Challenge

● Unscramble the word.

1. 

reab

____

2. 

bmilc

____

3. 

sdowo

____

● Listen and circle the correct word. MP3 11

4. She is (scared / tired) of dogs.

5. Don't (open / close) your eyes.

6. The (garden / ground) is wet from the rain.

Your Turn

● Draw and write about your friend.

Chapter 1

03 Molly's Friend, Charlie

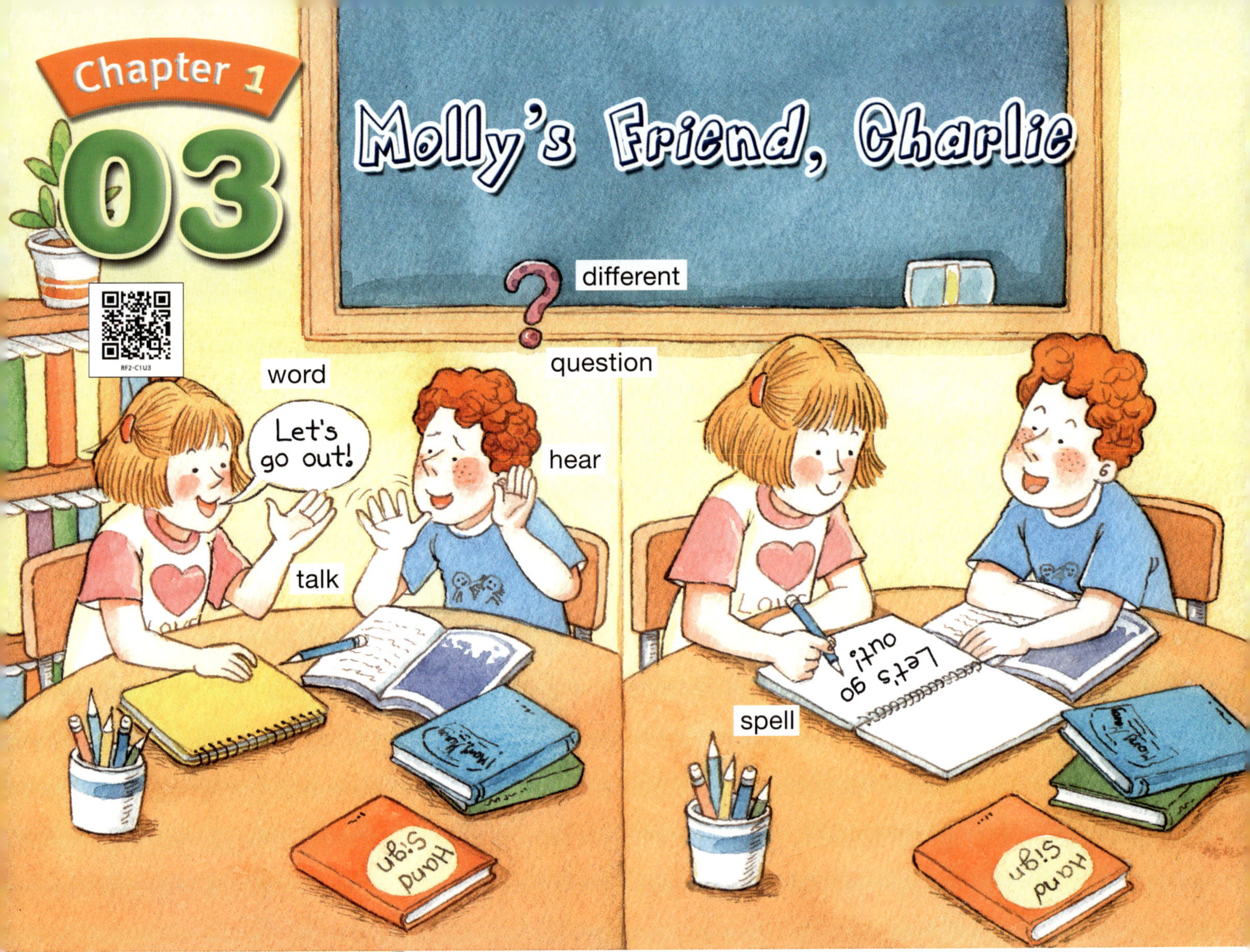

Get Ready

Look at the picture and talk about it.

1. What are the boy and the girl doing?
2. Are your friends like you or different from you?

Key Words

- Listen and write. MP3 12

1
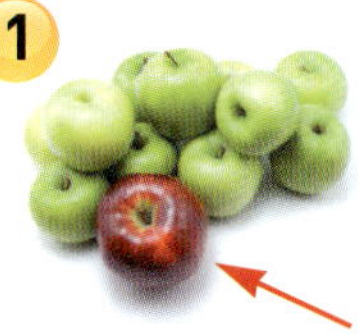
____

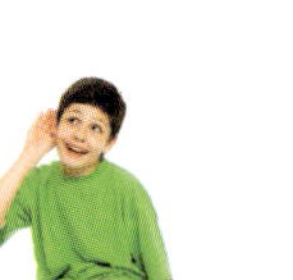

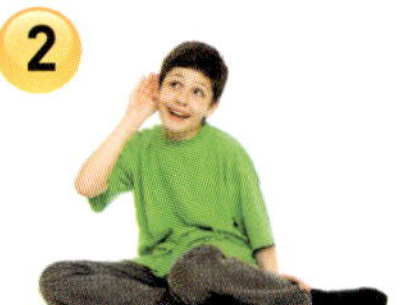

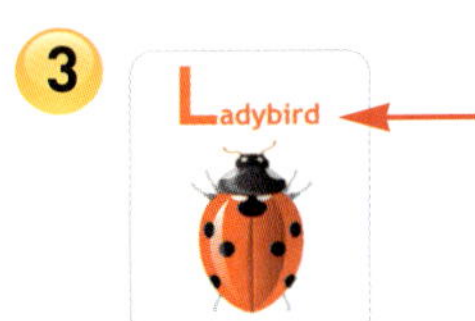

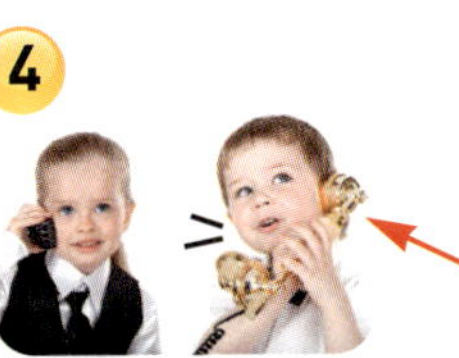

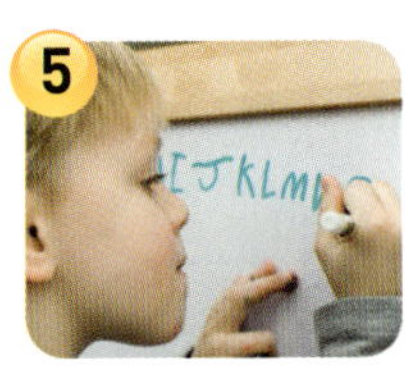

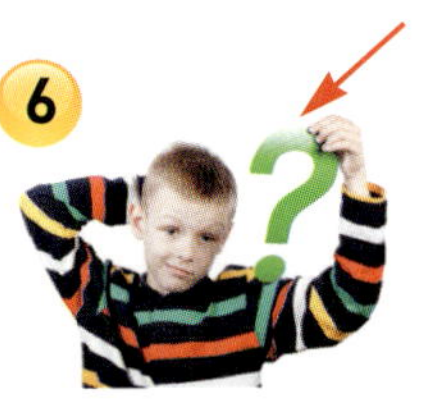

2
____

3

____

4
____

5
____

6
____

Are your friends like you?

Or are they **different** from you?

Molly lives in Canada.

She has a friend named Charlie.

Charlie can't **hear** **words**.

Molly uses her hands to **talk** to him.

She **spells** out words with her fingers.

Molly asks a **question**.

Charlie answers with his hands.

Then they look at each other and laugh.

Molly and Charlie are not the same.

But they are good friends.

Look!

- When two fingers and a thumb go up, it means, "I love you!" in sign language.

Check!

True False

1. Molly lives in Spain.
2. Molly can't hear words.
3. Molly and Charlie are good friends.

Reading Comprehension

● **Choose the best answer.**

1. What is the story about?

    a. Molly and Charlie   **b.** hearing words   **c.** using sign language

2. Charlie can't ___________ words.

    a. hear   **b.** see   **c.** say

3. Molly and Charlie are ___________ , but they are good friends.

    a. same   **b.** different   **c.** serious

4. What does Molly use to talk to Charlie?

    a.    **b.** 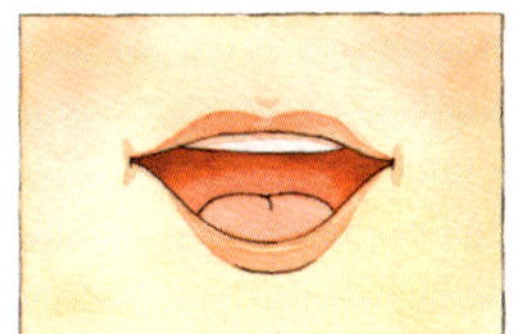   **c.** 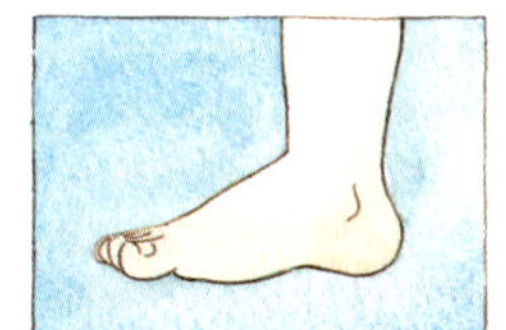

Reading Skills   Compare and Contrast

● **Fill in the chart.**

Word Challenge

● Match the opposite of each word.

1. talk   •   • hear

2. same   •   • answer

3. question   •   • different

● Listen and put an X on the wrong word. Write the correct word. 🎵 16

4. This is not a good idea.   _______________

5. He can't read his name.   _______________

6. She has flowers in her bag.   _______________

Your Turn

● Look at some letters in sign language. Then write the words.

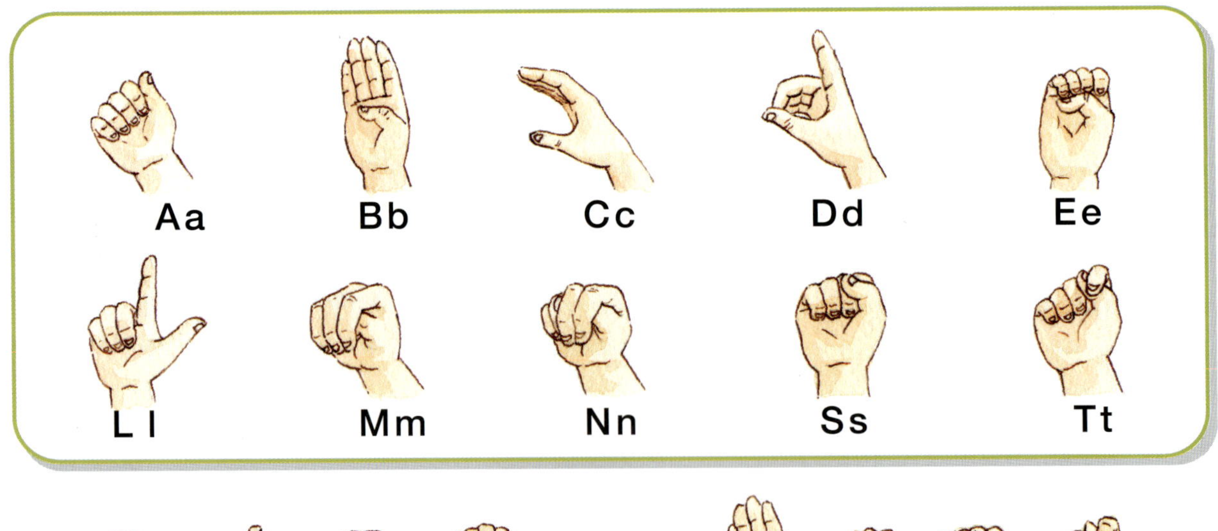

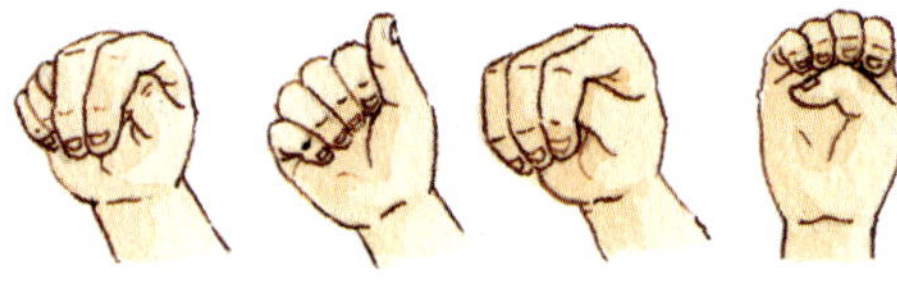

____

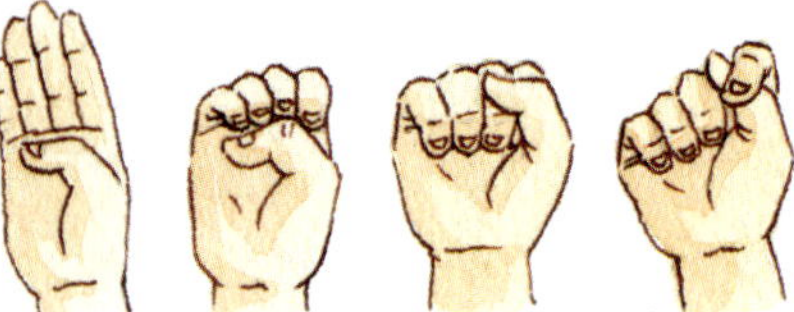

____

04

Are You a Good Friend?

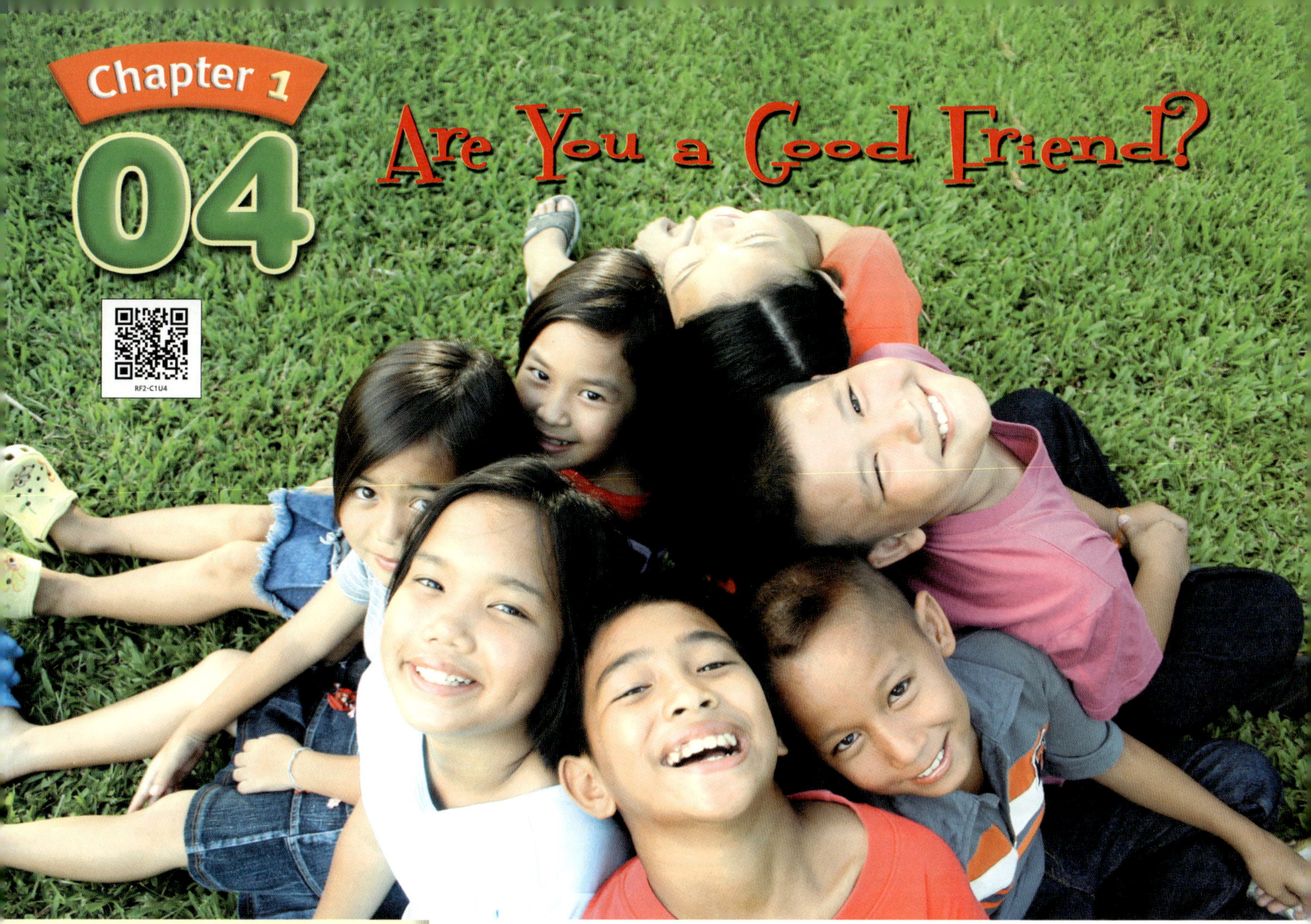

Get Ready

Look at the picture and talk about it.

1. What are the children doing?

2. What do you need to do to be a good friend?

Key Words

● **Listen and write.** MP3 17

| feel | cheer | help | laugh | fun | sad |

1. _______________

2. _______________

3. _______________

4. _______________

5. _______________

6. _______________

19

To be a good friend,

You need to do these things.

Have **fun**!

Do many things together with your friend.

Help your friend!

Be there with your friend when he needs you.

Cheer up your friend!

Make your friend **feel** better when he is **sad**.

Laugh with your friend!

Be happy for your friend when he is happy.

Try to be a good friend.

Your friend will be good to you!

Look!

- How many students are running in the picture?
- → ___________ students are running.

Check!

	True	False
1. You should have fun with your friend.	☐	☐
2. You should cheer up your friend.	☐	☐
3. Try to be a good friend first!	☐	☐

Reading Comprehension

● **Choose the best answer.**

1. What is the story about?
- **a.** being a good friend
- **b.** cheering up your friend
- **c.** laughing with your friend

2. _____________ your friend when he needs you.
- **a.** Beat
- **b.** Help
- **c.** Leave

3. When your friend is _____________, be happy for him.
- **a.** sad
- **b.** sick
- **c.** happy

4. Who are good friends?

a. 
b. 
c. 

Reading Skills   Identifying Details

● **Fill in the chart.**

How to Be a Good Friend

Have _______________!

_______________ your friend!

_______________ up your friend!

_______________ with your friend!

Word Challenge

● **Match each word with its meaning.**

1. help •
2. feel •
3. cheer •

• make easier or better
• make someone more hopeful
• experience a particular emotion

● **Listen and write the correct word.**  21

4. The party is _______________ .

5. The babies _______________ a lot.

6. He looks so _______________ today.

Your Turn

● **When do you feel sad and when do you feel happy? Write about it.**

Chapter 2

01 Happy Birthday, Mom!

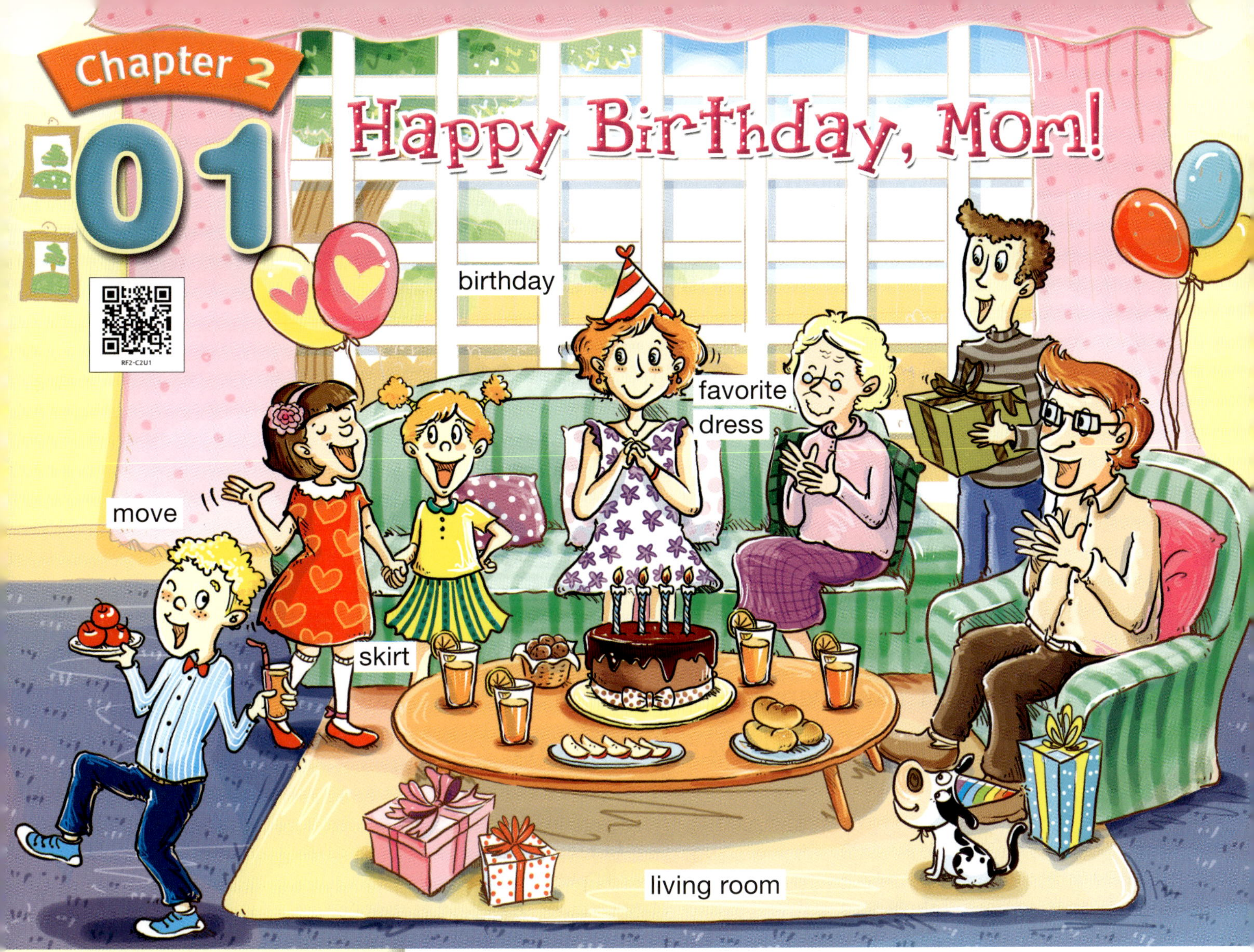

Get Ready

Look at the picture and talk about it.

1. Where are they?
2. What are they doing?

Key Words

- Listen and write. MP3 22

1 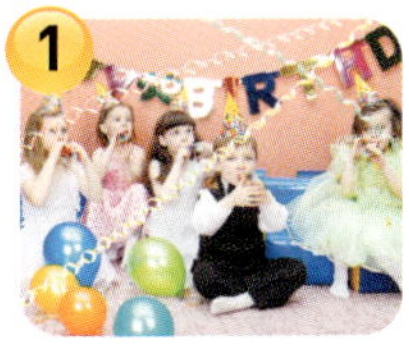
____

2
____

3
____

4
____

5
____

6
____

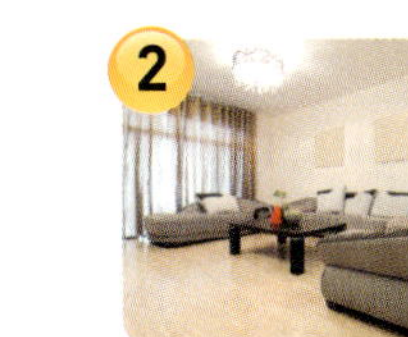

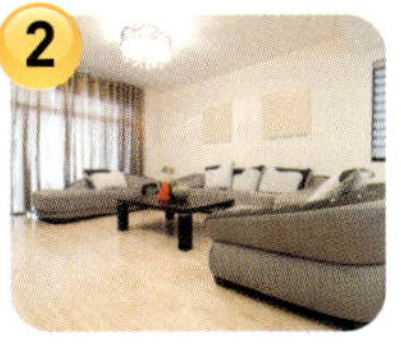

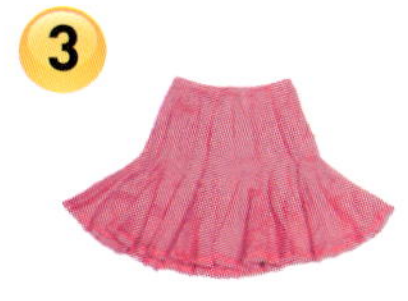

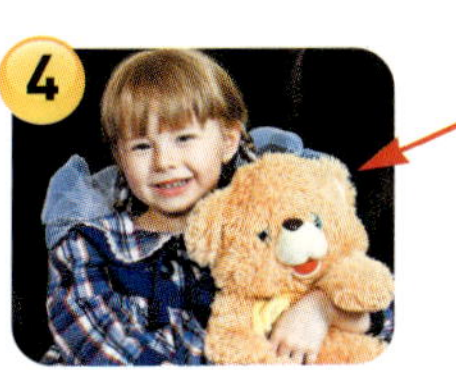

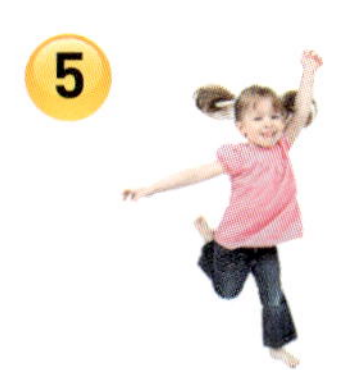

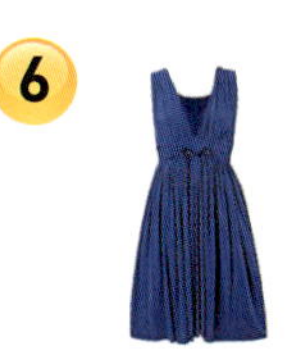

Look!

- How many hearts are in the picture?
→ There are __________ hearts.

Check!

	True	False
1. Today is dad's birthday.	☐	☐
2. Everyone is in the living room.	☐	☐
3. Sharon sings a song like grandma.		

Reading Comprehension

● **Choose the best answer.**

1. What is the story about?
   a. the family show
   b. the dance party
   c. the singing contest

2. Anna sings mom's ____________ song.
   a. hit
   b. favorite
   c. clapping

3. Who dances like dad?
   a. Anna
   b. Willy
   c. Sharon

4. What is Sharon wearing?
   a. 
   b. 
   c. 

Reading Skills   Identifying Characters

● **Fill in the chart.**

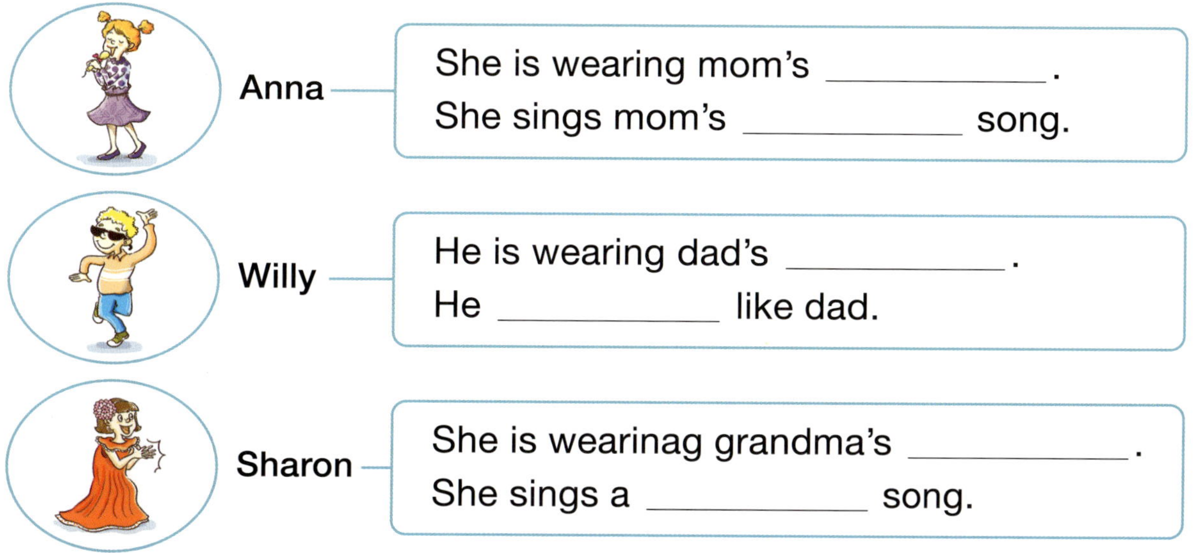

Word Challenge

● **Complete the word.**

1. 

bir☐☐day

2. 

☐☐irt

3. 

dre☐☐

● **Listen and write the correct word.** MP3 26

4. She is in the _________________ .

5. I can't _________________ around much.

6. This is my dad's _________________ book.

Your Turn

● **Draw and describe your friends' items.**

This is <u>Amy's</u> skirt.

This is _________ shirt.

These are _________ sunglasses.

These are _________ gloves.

This is _________ dress.

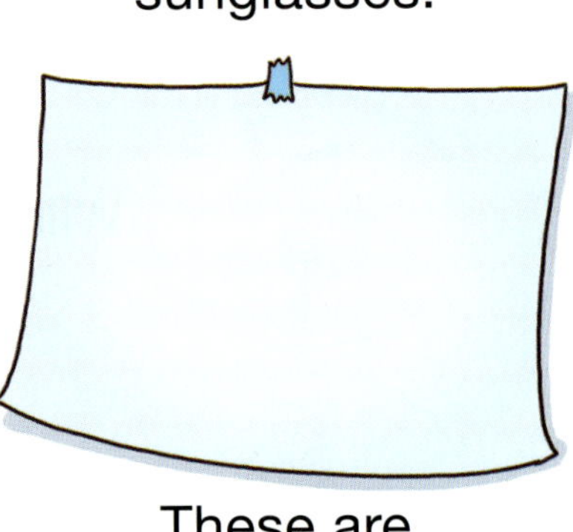

These are _________ boots.

Chapter 2

02 The Baseball Game

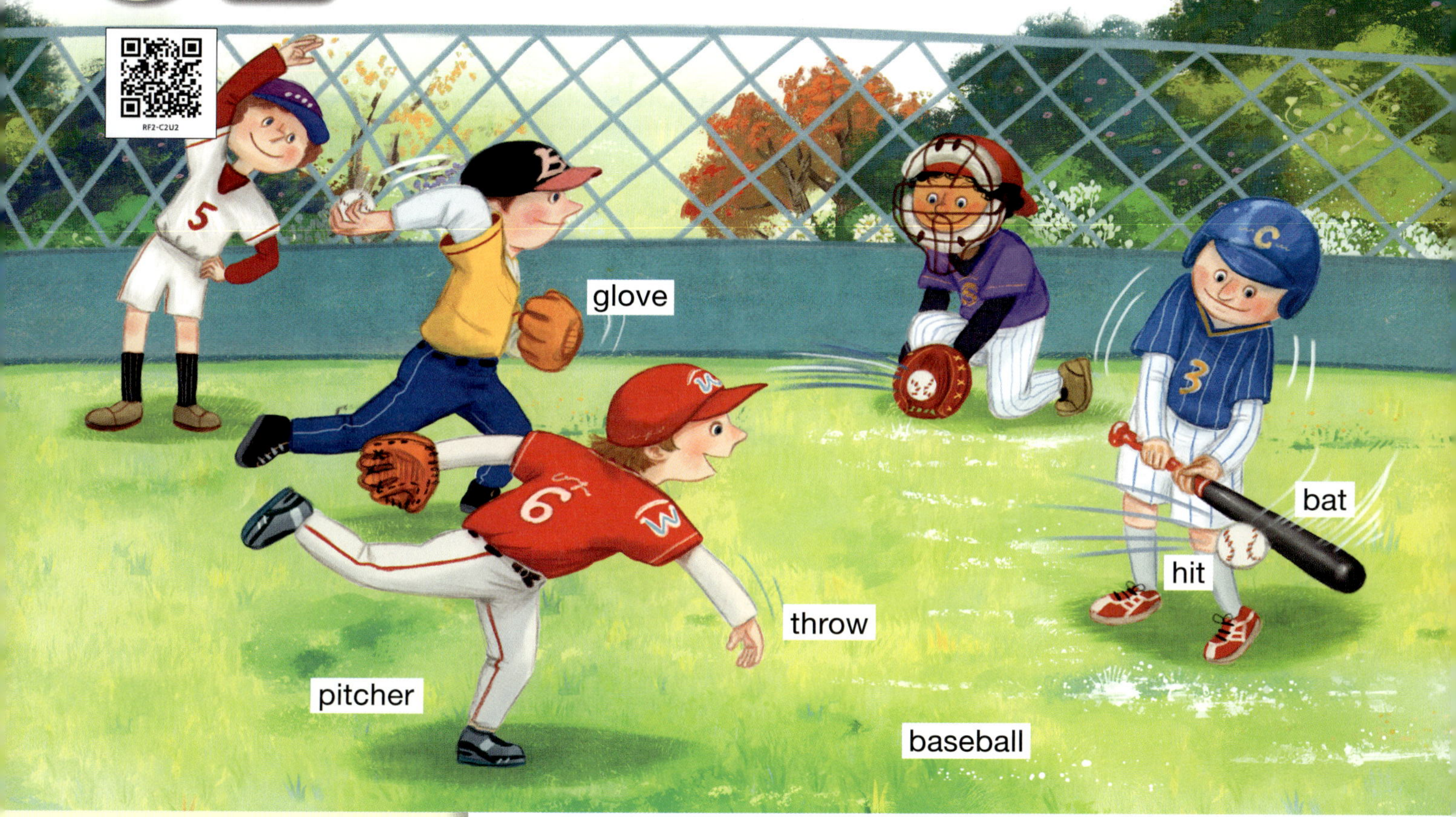

Get Ready

Look at the picture and talk about it.

1. What do you see in the picture?
2. What do we need to play baseball?

Key Words

Listen and write. MP3 27

1 ______________

2 ______________

3 ______________

4 ______________

5 ______________

6 ______________

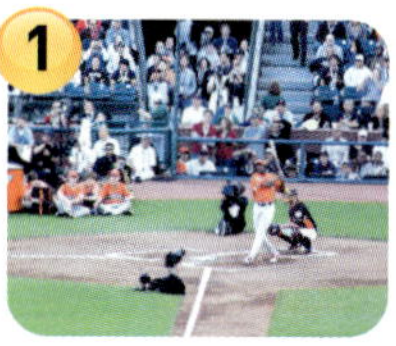

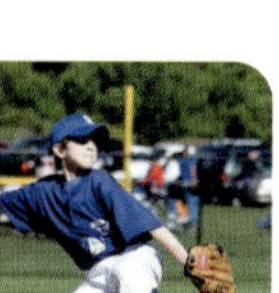

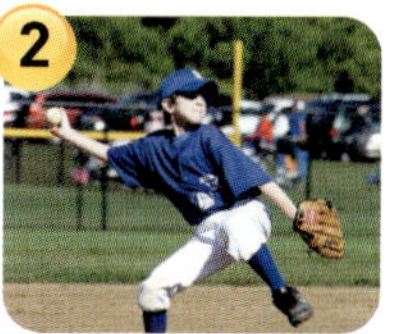

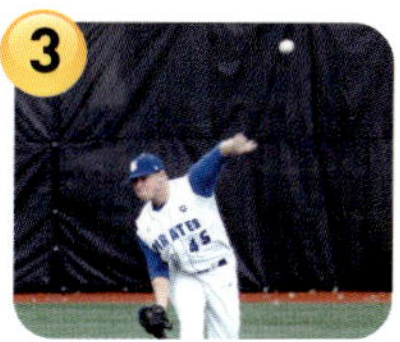

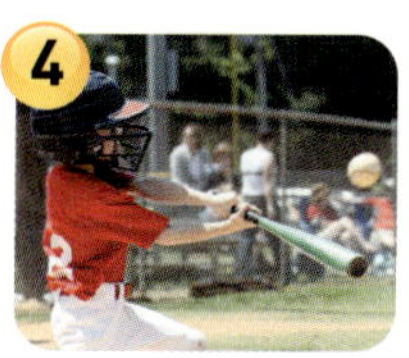

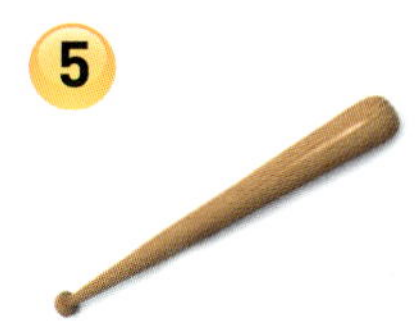

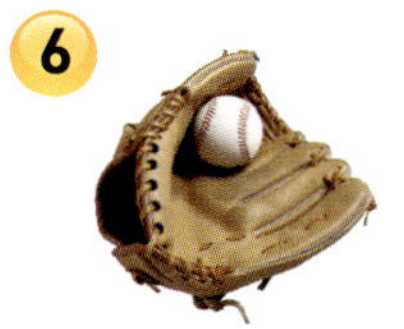

Children are playing baseball today.

Ben, Dennis, and Richard are on the field.

Ben is a pitcher.

Whoosh! He throws the ball.

Dennis is a hitter.

Rap! He hits the ball with his bat.

Richard is a catcher.

Plump! He catches the ball with his glove.

Whoever gets three strikes is out!

Strike! One! Two! Three!

Dennis is out!

Now, who is the next hitter?

Look!

- What number is player Ben?
- → He is number

  __________ .

Check!

1. Children are playing basketball.
2. Dennis is a hitter.
3. Whoever gets two strikes is out.

True False

Reading Comprehension

● **Choose the best answer.**

1. What is the story about?
- **a.** playing a board game
- **b.** playing a baseball game
- **c.** playing a ping pong game

2. Who is a pitcher?
- **a.** Ben
- **b.** Dennis
- **c.** Richard

3. Richard ______________ the ball with his glove.
- **a.** throws
- **b.** hits
- **c.** catches

4. Who gets three strikes?

a.    **b.**    **c.** 

Reading Skills   Identifying Characters

● **Fill in the chart.**

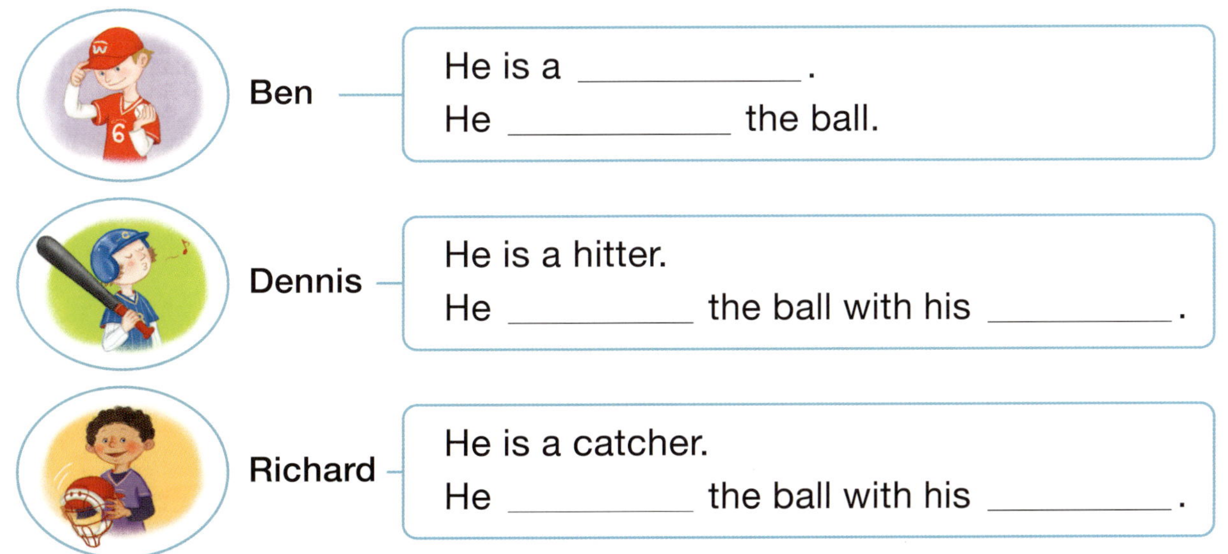

Ben — He is a ______________.
He ______________ the ball.

Dennis — He is a hitter.
He ______________ the ball with his ______________.

Richard — He is a catcher.
He ______________ the ball with his ______________.

Word Challenge

● Unscramble the word.

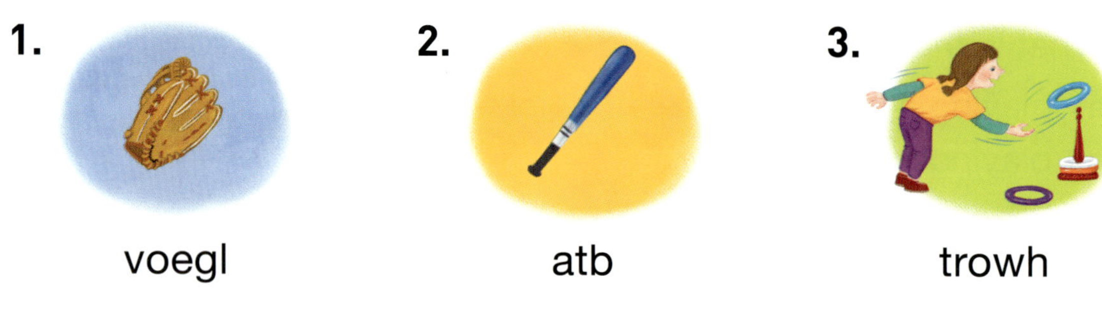

1. voegl

2. atb

3. trowh

_______   _______   _______

● Listen and circle the correct word. 31

4. Don't (hit / kick) the ball.

5. He is a good (catcher / pitcher) in our team.

6. They are watching (baseball / tennis) on TV.

Your Turn

● Draw a catcher, a pitcher, and a hitter on the baseball field. Then talk about how to play baseball.

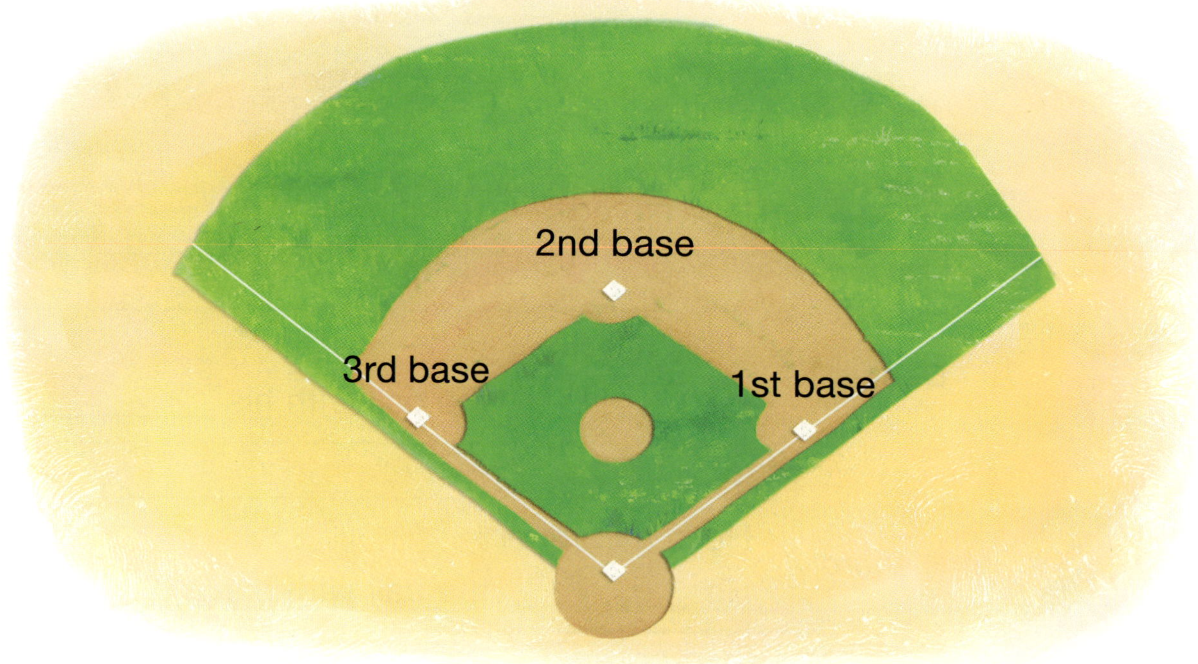

Chapter 2

03 Manners at Classical Concerts

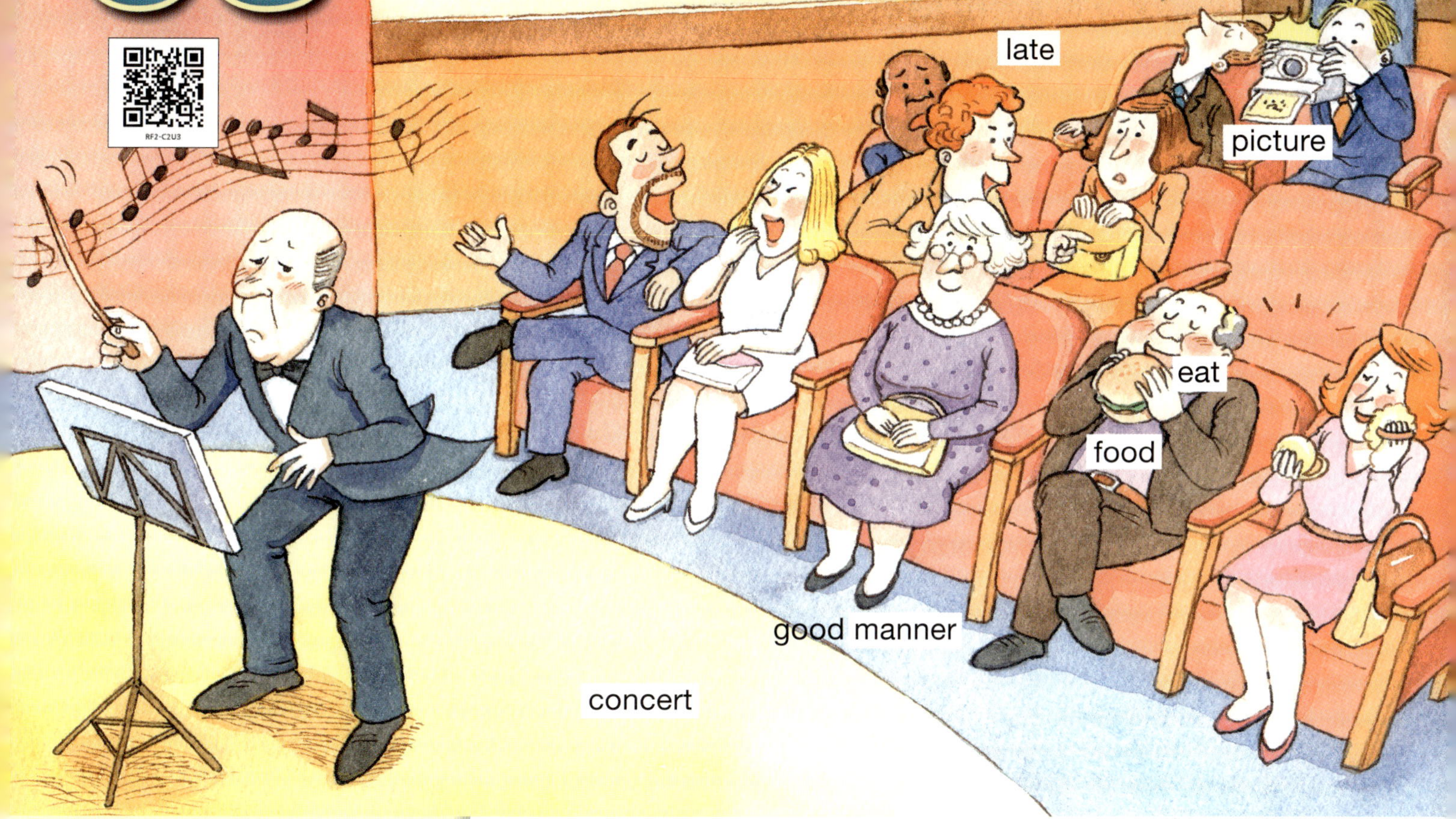

Get Ready

Look at the picture and talk about it.

1. Where are they?

2. What are good manners at classical concerts?

Key Words

● **Listen and write.** MP3 32

1

____

2

____

3 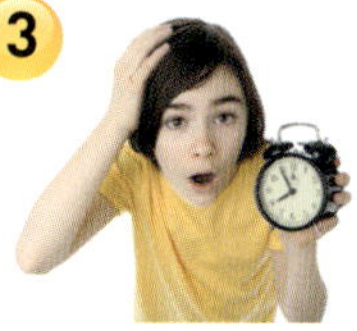

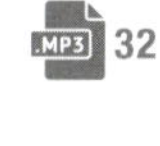

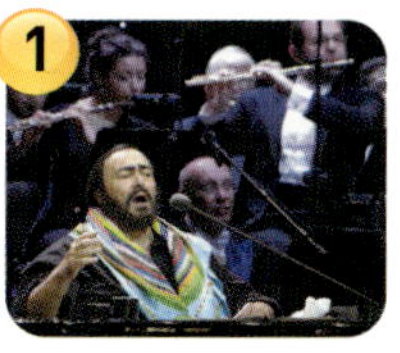

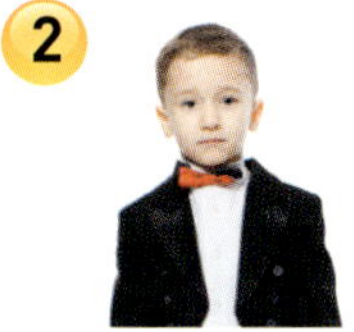

____

4

____

5

____

6

____

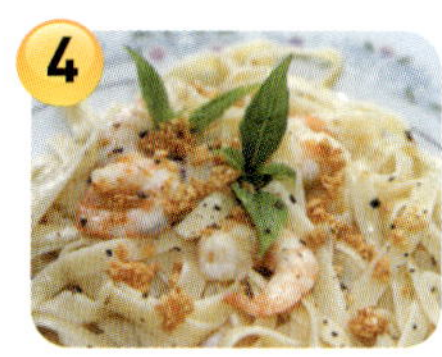

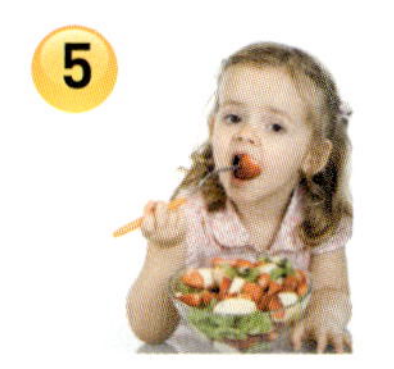

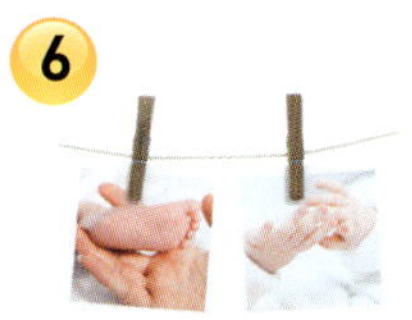

Do you like classical **concerts**?

They are very formal.

We need to use good **manners**.

First, we should not be **late**!

When the concert starts, the doors close.

We need to be there early.

Second, we should be quiet!

Shhh! We should not talk.

Others want to listen to music.

Third, we should not bring **food**!

We can't **eat** inside.

And we should not take **pictures**, either!

Look!

- How many people are watching the concert?

→ ___________ people are watching the concert.

Check!

		True	False
1.	Classical concerts are very formal.	☐	☐
2.	We need to use good manners.	☐	☐
3.	We can bring food at a classical concert.	☐	☐

Reading Comprehension

● **Choose the best answer.**

1. What is the story about?
   a. Manners in the library
   b. Manners in public places
   c. Manners at classical concerts

2. We should not be ____________ for classical concerts.

   a. early   **b.** late   **c.** quiet

3. We should not ____________ pictures during classical concerts.

   a. use   **b.** bring   **c.** take

4. Who has good classical concert manners?

   a.    **b.**    **c.** 

Reading Skills   Identifying Details

● **Fill in the chart.**

Manners at Classical Concerts

1. We should not be ________________ !

2. We should be ________________ !

3. We should not ________________ food!

4. We should not ________________ pictures!

Word Challenge

● **Check the correct word for each picture.**

1. 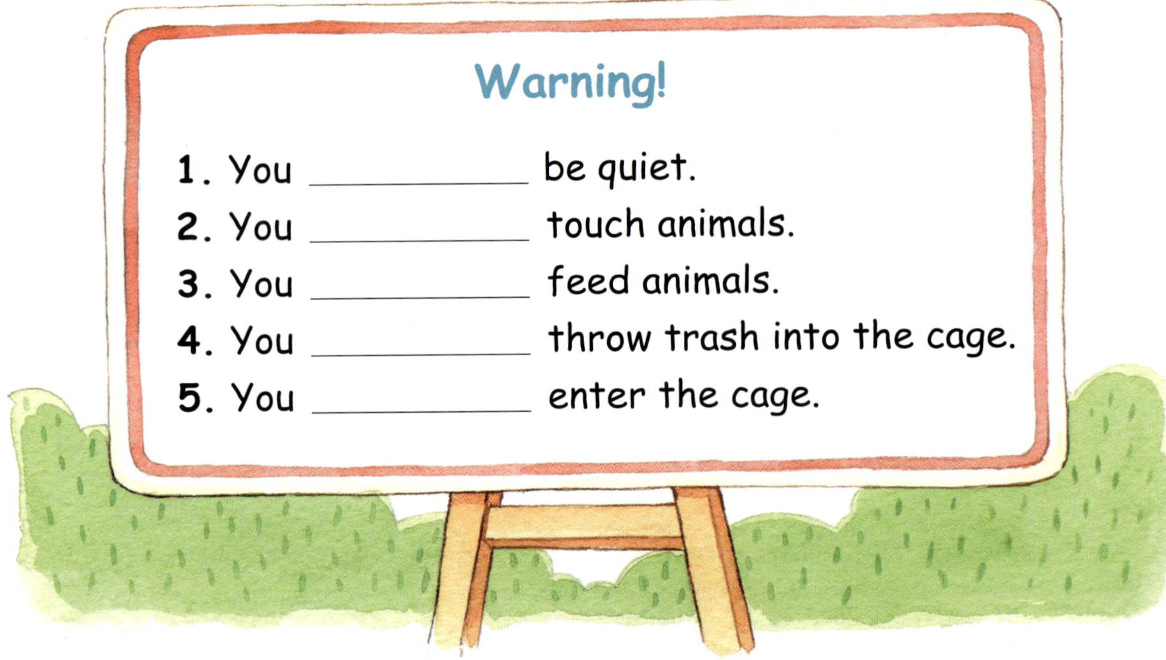

☐ good
☐ food

2.

☐ hate
☐ late

3.

☐ eat
☐ meat

● **Listen and put an X on the wrong word. Write the correct word.** 🔊 36

4. He has good sense. ________________

5. They are watching a movie. ________________

6. She is looking at the window. ________________

Your Turn

● **Look at the memo at the national zoo. Then fill in the blank with "should" or "should not".**

Chapter 2

04 Folk Dancing

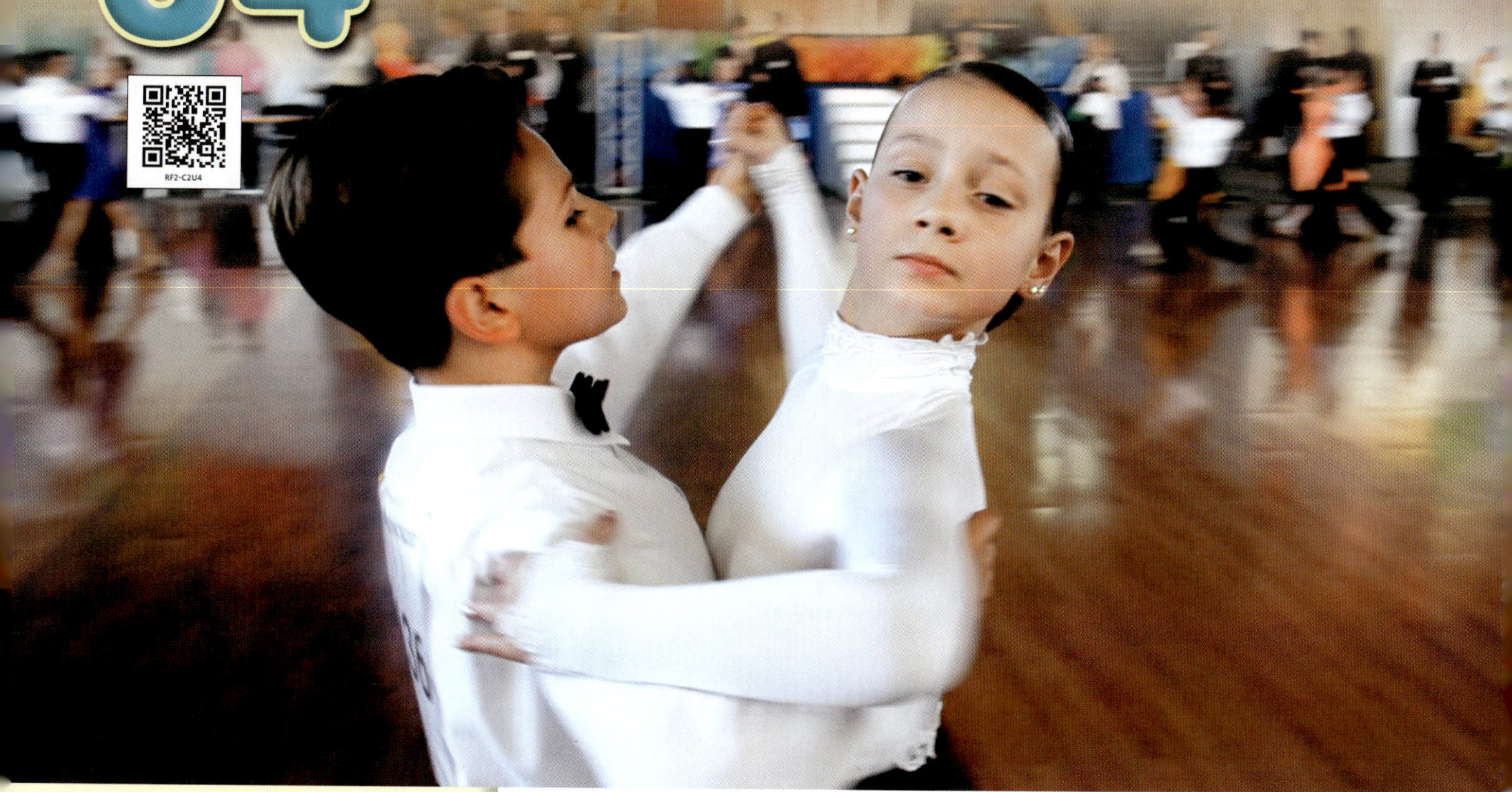

RF2-C2U4

Get Ready

Look at the picture and talk about it.

1. What are the boy and the girl doing?
2. What kind of dance do you like to learn?

Key Words

- Listen and write. MP3 37

feet	spin	stamp	clap	music	step

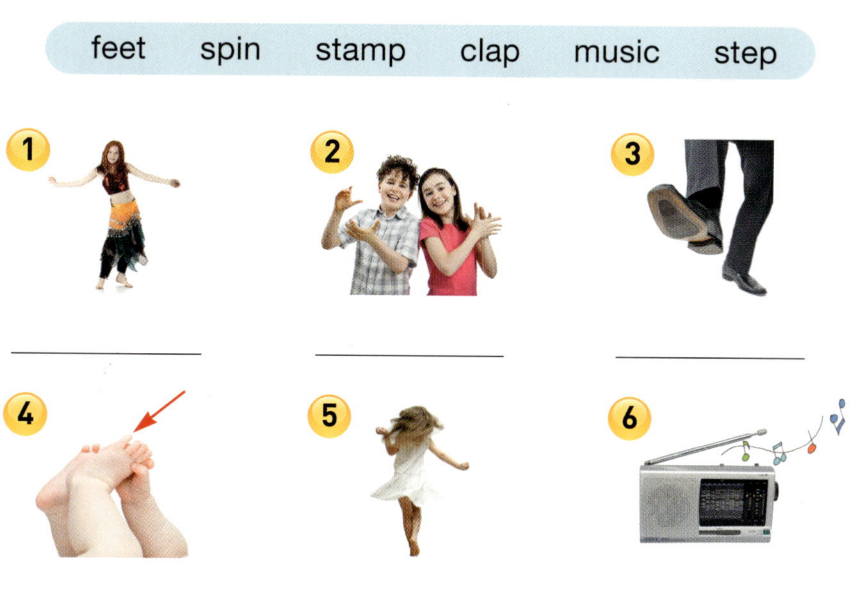

1 ____________

2 ____________

3 ____________

4 ____________

5 ____________

6 ____________

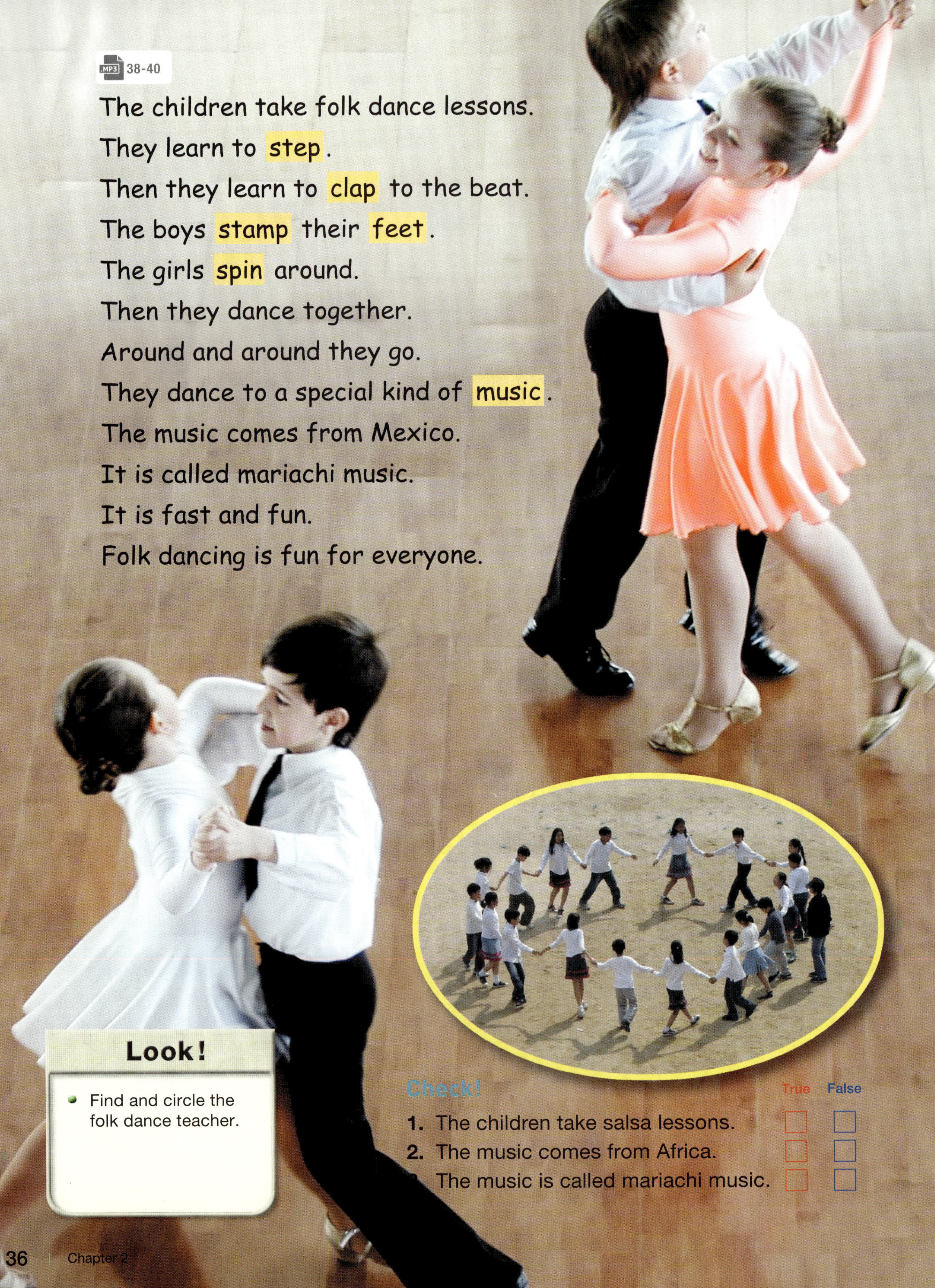

The children take folk dance lessons.

They learn to **step**.

Then they learn to **clap** to the beat.

The boys **stamp** their **feet**.

The girls **spin** around.

Then they dance together.

Around and around they go.

They dance to a special kind of **music**.

The music comes from Mexico.

It is called mariachi music.

It is fast and fun.

Folk dancing is fun for everyone.

Look!

- Find and circle the folk dance teacher.

Check!

    True   False

1. The children take salsa lessons.
2. The music comes from Africa.
   The music is called mariachi music.

Reading Comprehension

● **Choose the best answer.**

1. What is the story about?
- **a.** the dance festival
- **b.** learning folk dance
- **c.** listening to special music

2. The children learn to _____________ and clap to the beat.
- **a.** hop
- **b.** jump
- **c.** step

3. The folk dancing is _____________ for everyone.
- **a.** easy
- **b.** fun
- **c.** fast

4. What kind of lessons do children take?

a. 　　**b.** 　　**c.** 

Reading Skills Sequencing

● **Number the pictures in the order of learning folk dance.**

Word Challenge

● **Match each word with its meaning.**

1. clap	•	•	turn around very quickly
2. step	•	•	hit your hands against each other
3. spin	•	•	lift your foot and put it down very hard
4. stamp	•	•	lift your foot and put it down in a different place

● **Listen and write the correct word.** `MP3` 41

5. I like to listen to _________________.

6. He has long legs and big _________________.

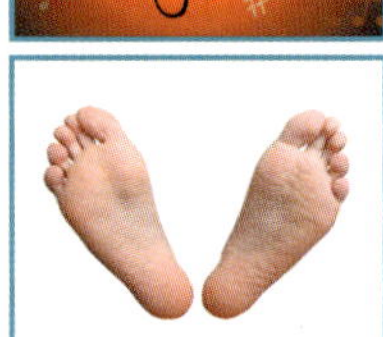

Your Turn

● **Make a sign-up form for folk dancing class.**

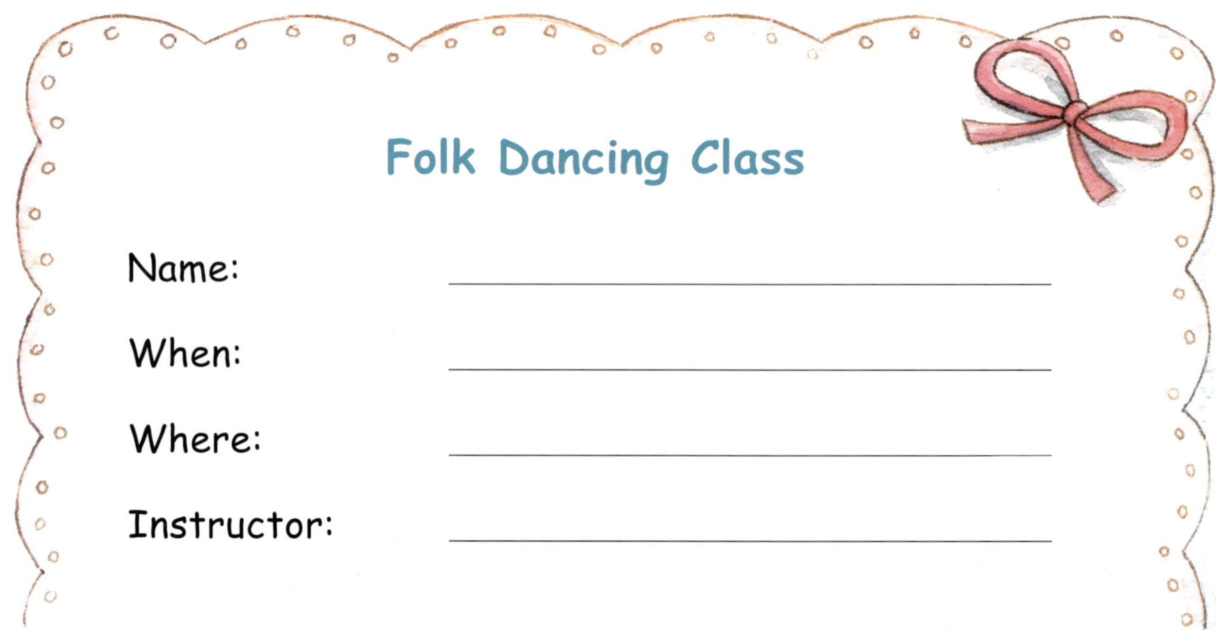

Chapter 3

01 Little Tomatoes

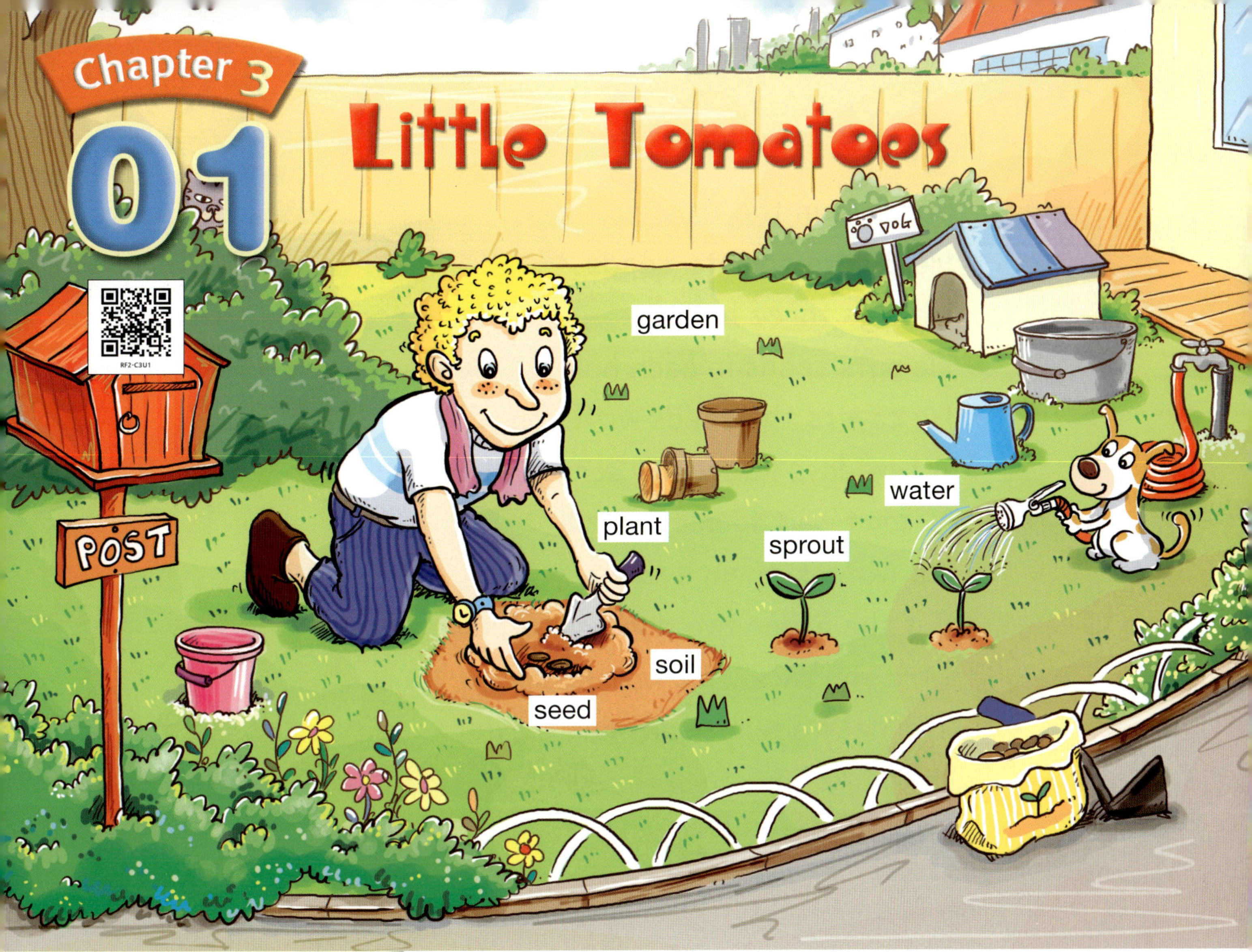

Get Ready

Look at the picture and talk about it.

1. What is the boy doing?
2. What do plants need to grow?

Key Words

Listen and write. MP3 42

1 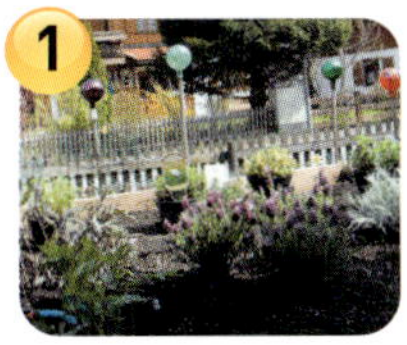

______

2

______

3

______

4

______

5

______

6 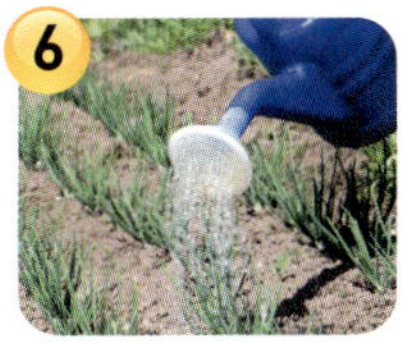

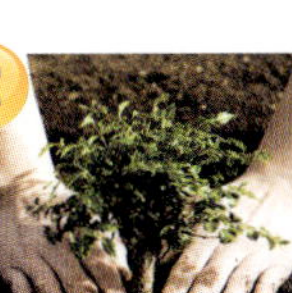

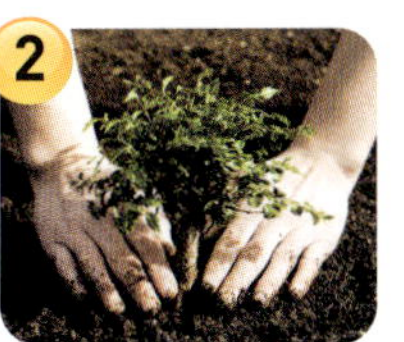

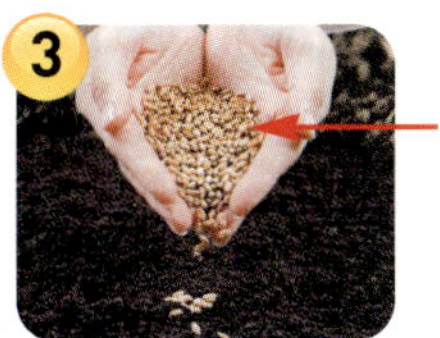

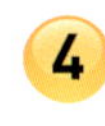

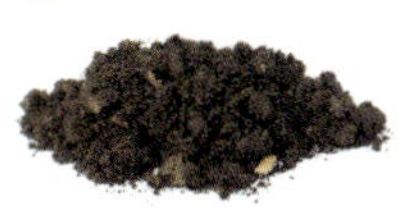

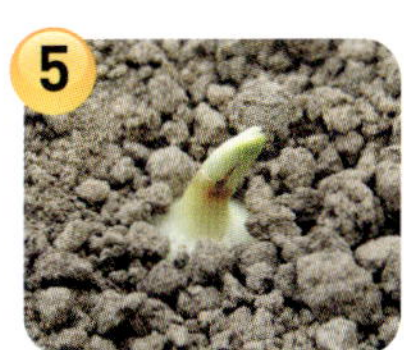

______

Jacob is in the garden.

He plants tomato seeds.

He digs three holes.

He puts seeds in each hole.

He covers the seeds with soil.

A few days later, one sprout shows up.

"I can't wait to see you all!"

He waters them every day.

But the other two don't come out.

"Are you okay?" he worries.

The next day, he sees new sprouts.

"Hi, little tomato sprouts!"

Look!

- How many sprouts do you see in the picture?
- → There are __________ sprouts.

Check!

	True	False
1. Jacob is in the park.	☐	☐
2. Jacob plants potato seeds.	☐	☐
3. Jacob worries when two sprouts don't come out.	☐	☐

Reading Comprehension

● **Choose the best answer.**

1. What is the story about?
- **a.** watering the garden
- **b.** digging three holes in the garden
- **c.** growing tomato seeds in the garden

2. Jacob _____________ three holes and _____________ seeds in each hole.
- **a.** digs - covers
- **b.** digs - puts
- **c.** plants - puts

3. Jacob waters the tomato seeds _____________.
- **a.** every hour
- **b.** every day
- **c.** every week

4. What does Jacob see in the garden when he says, "Hi, little tomato sprouts!"?

a. 
b. 
c. 

Reading Skills   Summarizing

● **Fill in the chart.**

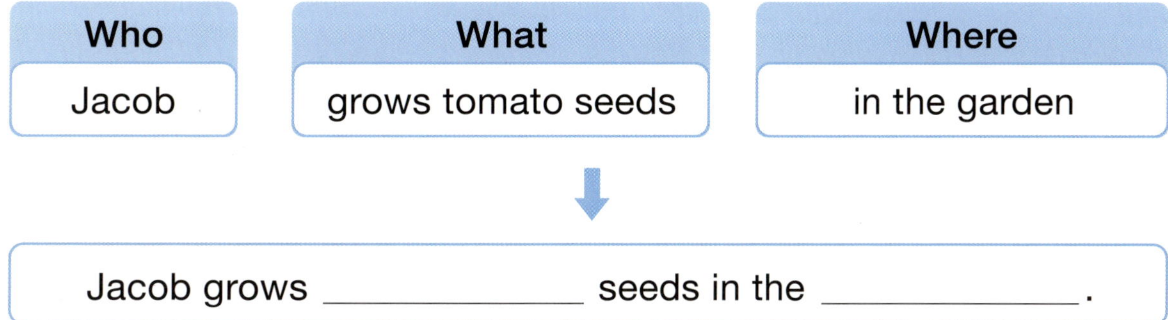

Who	What	Where
Jacob	grows tomato seeds	in the garden

Jacob grows _____________ seeds in the _____________.

Word Challenge

● **Complete the word.**

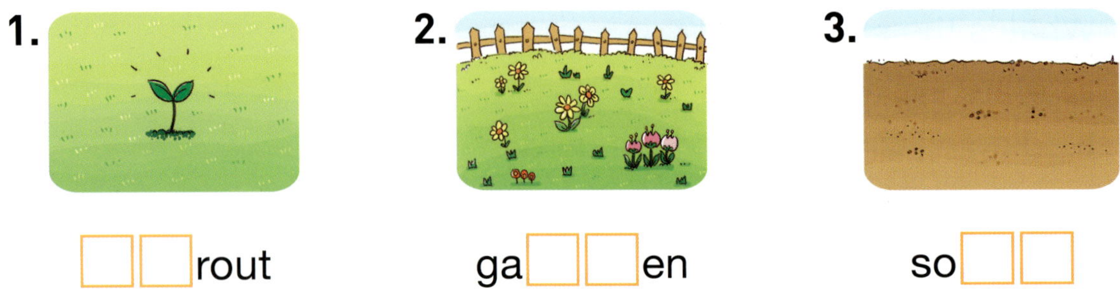

1. ☐☐rout

2. ga☐☐en

3. so☐☐

● **Listen and write the correct word.** 🎵 46

4. We _________________ trees every year.

5. A tomato grows up from a _________________ .

6. Do you like to _________________ the flowers?

Your Turn

● **Draw the missing picture and tell the story.**

Chapter 3

02 Yummy Apple!

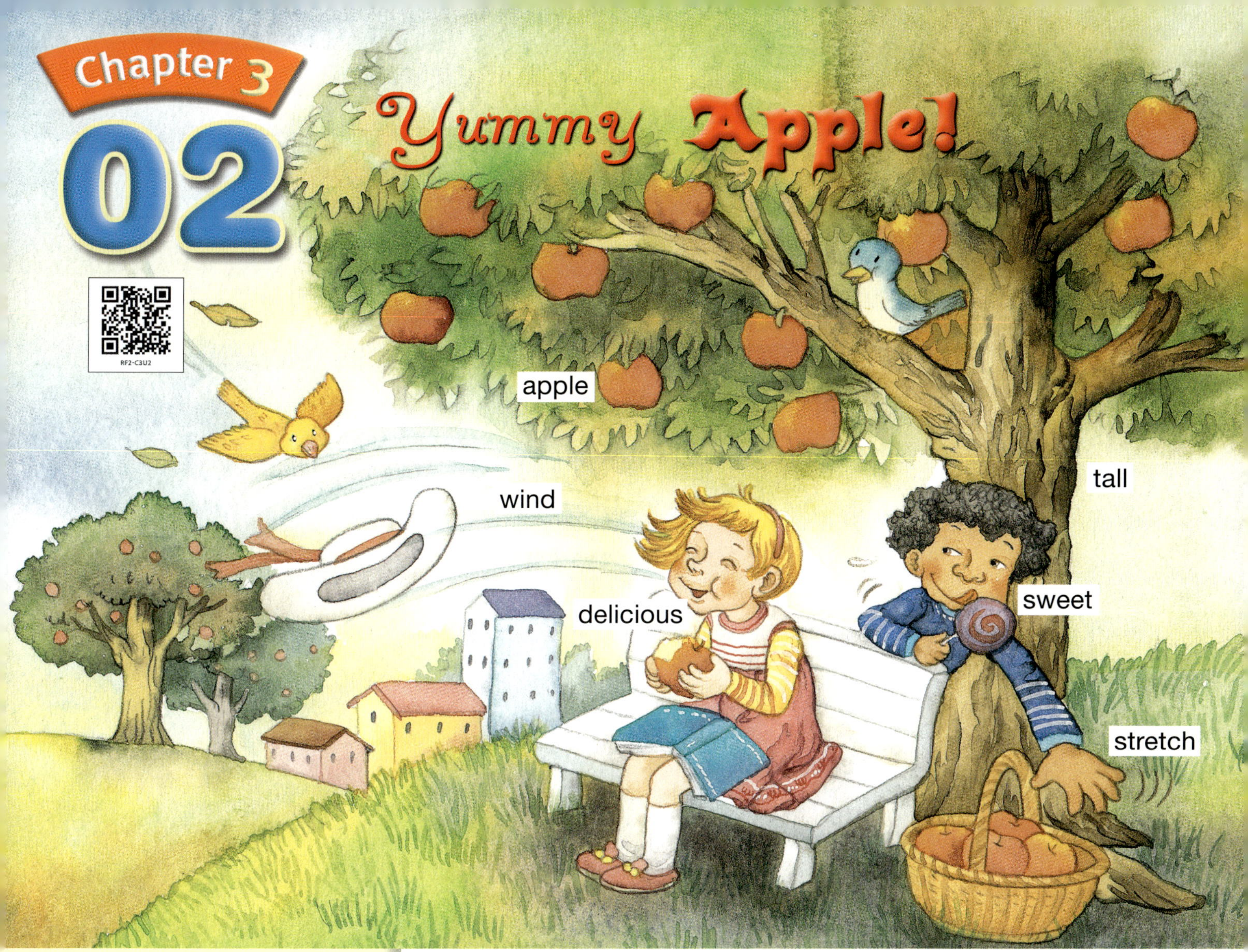

Get Ready

Look at the picture and talk about it.

1. Where are the boy and the girl?
2. What is the boy doing?

Key Words

● Listen and write. MP3 47

1 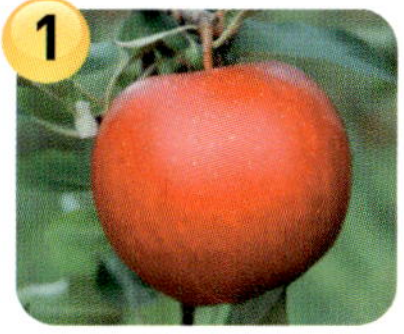 ______

2 ______

3 ______

4 ______

5 ______

6 ______

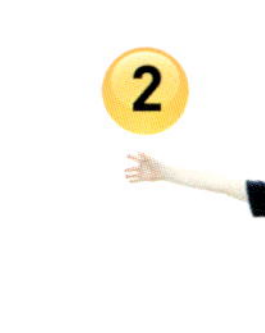

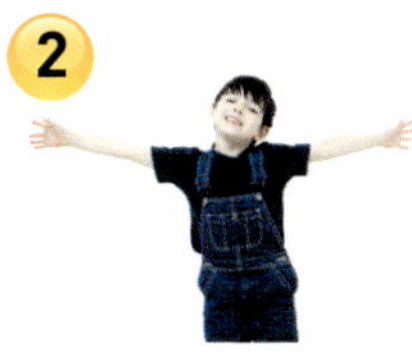

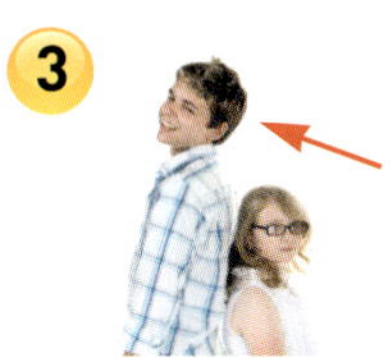

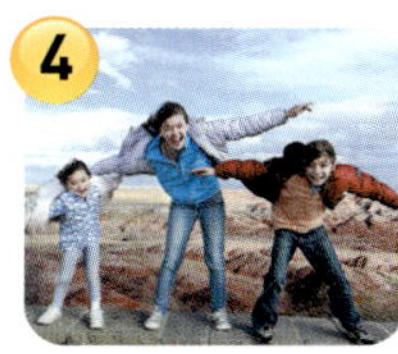

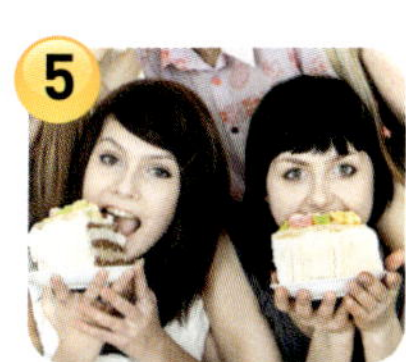

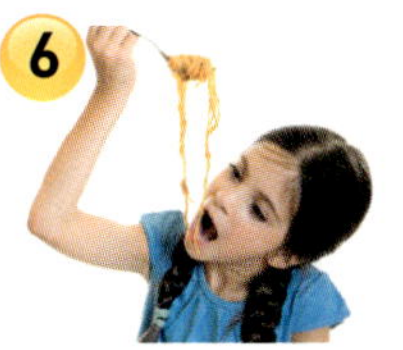

Look!

- How many apples do you see on the tree?
→ There are __________ apples.

Check!

		True	False
1.	Janet is under the apple tree.	☐	☐
2.	Janet stretches her arms to reach the apples.	☐	☐
3.	Janet picks up the green apple.	☐	☐

Reading Comprehension

● **Choose the best answer.**

1. What is the story about?
   a. the apple farm
   b. picking apples
   c. a delicious apple

2. The apple tree is too _____________ .
   a. big   **b.** round   **c.** tall

3. How does Janet's apple look?
   a. sweet   **b.** sour   **c.** bitter

4. Where is Janet hit?

a.    **b.**    **c.** 

Reading Skills   Cause and Effect

● **Fill in the chart.**

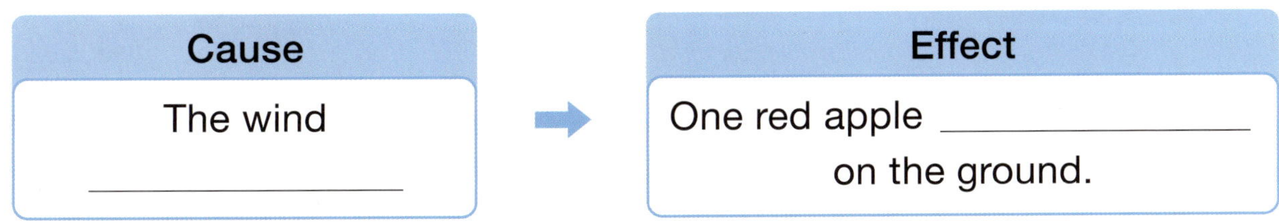

Cause		Effect
The wind _____________	➡	One red apple _____________ on the ground.

Word Challenge

● Unscramble the word.

1.

tehrcts

____

2.

palpe

____

3.

lsciuiedo

____

● Listen and circle the correct word. [MP3] 51

4. Do you like (hot / sweet) food?

5. He is (tall / thin) and handsome.

6. I don't want to go out in the (rain / wind).

Your Turn

● Look at the pictures and describe them.

The bag is too small.

The man is ________ ________.

The shelf is

________ ________.

The boy is

________ ________.

The shirt is

________ ________.

03 HOW OLD IS THE TREE?

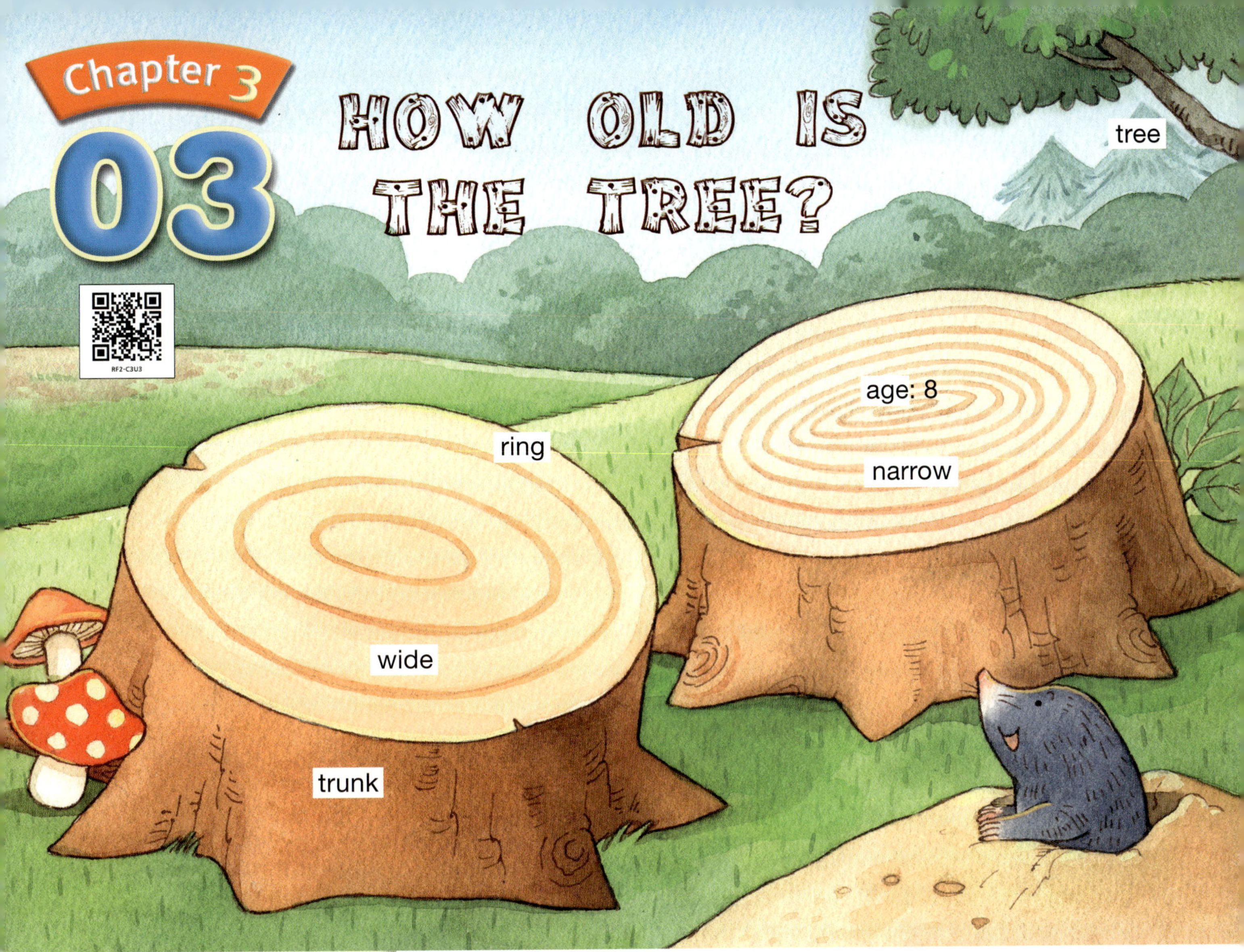

Get Ready

Look at the picture and talk about it.

1. What do you see in the picture?

2. How do you find the age of a tree?

Key Words

● Listen and write. MP3 52

1

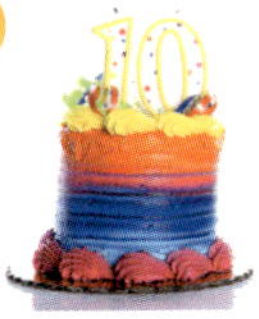

2

3

4

5

6

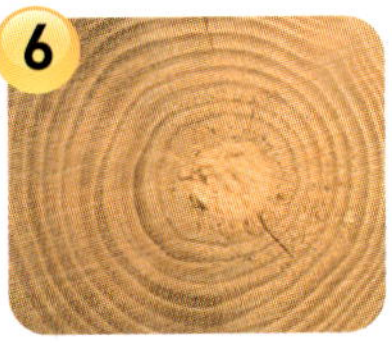

How old are you?

The answer is easy!

How do you find the age of a tree?

There is an easy way, too!

First, look at the trunk of a tree.

You will see many circles.

Some circles are wide.

Some circles are narrow.

These circles are called rings.

Second, count all the rings.

Each ring equals one year.

How old is a tree with 100 rings?

Look!

- How many rings do you see on the tree trunk?
- → There are __________ rings.

Check!

1. It's easy to find the age of a tree.
2. The circles on a tree trunk are called rings.
3. Each ring equals one year.

True False

Reading Comprehension

Choose the best answer.

1. What is the story about?
- **a.** the age of a tree
- **b.** the trunk of a tree
- **c.** different shapes of rings

2. Rings tell us _____________ a tree is.
- **a.** how old
- **b.** how narrow
- **c.** how wide

3. One ring equals _____________ year.
- **a.** one
- **b.** five
- **c.** ten

4. Which tree trunk is five years old?

a.  **b.**  **c.** 

Reading Skills Sequencing

Fill in the chart.

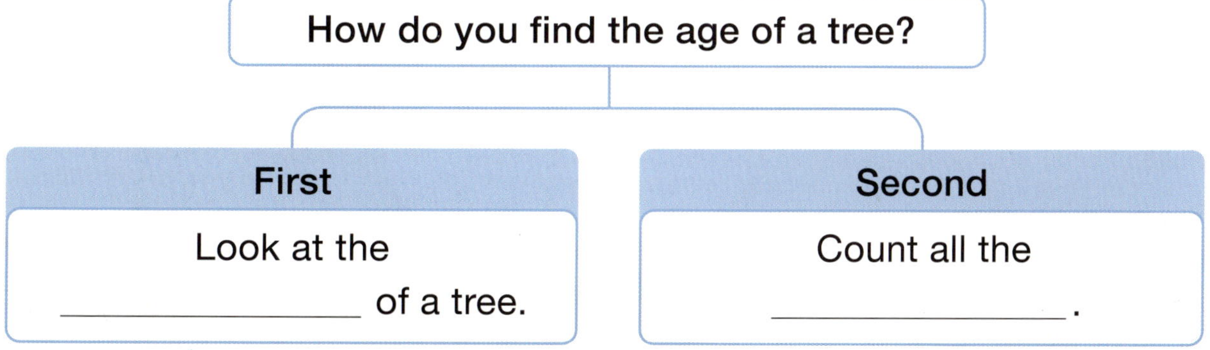

How do you find the age of a tree?

First	Second
Look at the _____________ of a tree.	Count all the _____________.

Word Challenge

- **Check the correct word for each picture.**

1. ☐ hide
☐ wide

2. ☐ free
☐ tree

3. ☐ ring
☐ sing

- **Listen and put an X on the wrong word. Write the correct word.** .MP3 56

4. The road is too long. ______________________

5. I don't know your name. ______________________

6. He sits on a tree branch. ______________________

Your Turn

- **Draw rings on each tree trunk and talk about them.**

04 What are Some Parts of Plants?

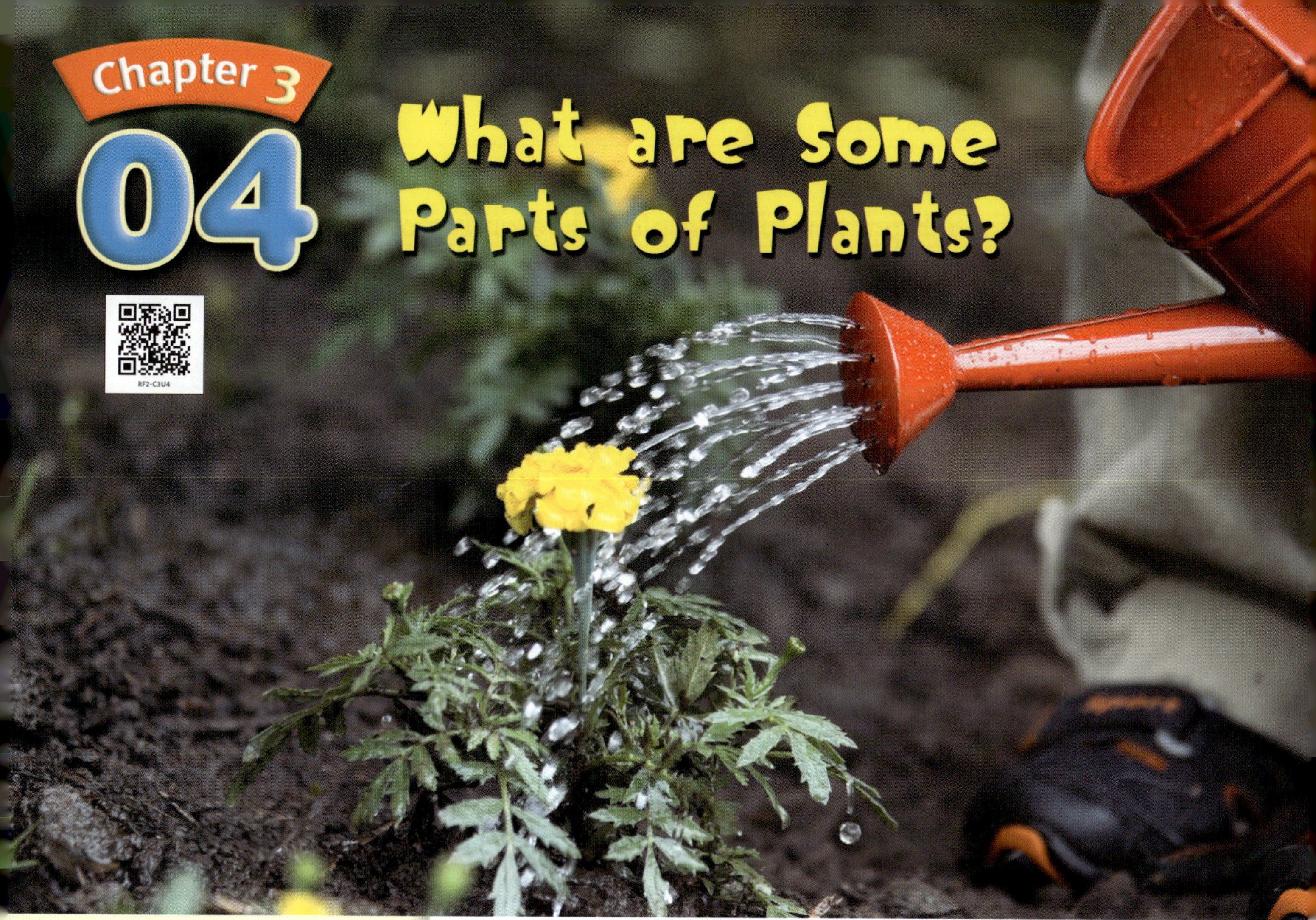

Get Ready

Look at the picture and talk about it.

1. What do you see in the picture?

2. What are some parts of plants?

Key Words

● **Listen and write.** 🎵 57

| stem | leaf | air | flower | light | root |

1 

2

3

4

5

6

MP3 58-60

Plants have different parts.
Each part helps the plant live and grow.
Roots hold the plant in the soil.
They take in water.
Stems take water from the roots.
They carry water to other parts.
Leaves collect light and air.
They make food for the plant.
Plants also have flowers.
Flowers make seeds.
Now, you know all parts of a plant
and what each part does.

Look!

- Look at the picture of the plant and fill in the blanks.

Check!

	True	False
1. Plants have three different parts.		
2. Stems take water from the roots.		
3. Each part is important for the plant.		

Reading Comprehension

Choose the best answer.

1. What is the story about?

   a. how plants live   **b.** some parts of plants **c.** what plants need

2. What part holds the plant in the soil?

   a. root   **b.** stem   **c.** leaf

3. What part of a plant carries water to other parts?

   a. stem   **b.** leaf   **c.** flower

4. What part of a plant makes seeds?

a.    **b.**    **c.** 

Reading Skills   Identifying Details

Fill in the chart.

Parts of a Plant and What Each Part Does

- Roots _____________ the plant in the soil and take in _____________ .
- Stems take water from the _____________ and _____________ it to other parts.
- Leaves collect light and _____________ and make _____________ for the plant.
- Flowers make _____________ .

Word Challenge

- **Cross out the unrelated word.**

1.  | Plant Part | root | leaf | tail

2. What plants need | light | rock | water

- **Listen and write the correct word.** .MP3 61

3. He is enjoying the fresh _____________.

4. This _____________ has a bright color.

5. The _____________ of this plant is very thin.

Your Turn

- **Draw your favorite plant. Then write the names of the different parts of the plant.**

Chapter 4

01 My Piggy Bank

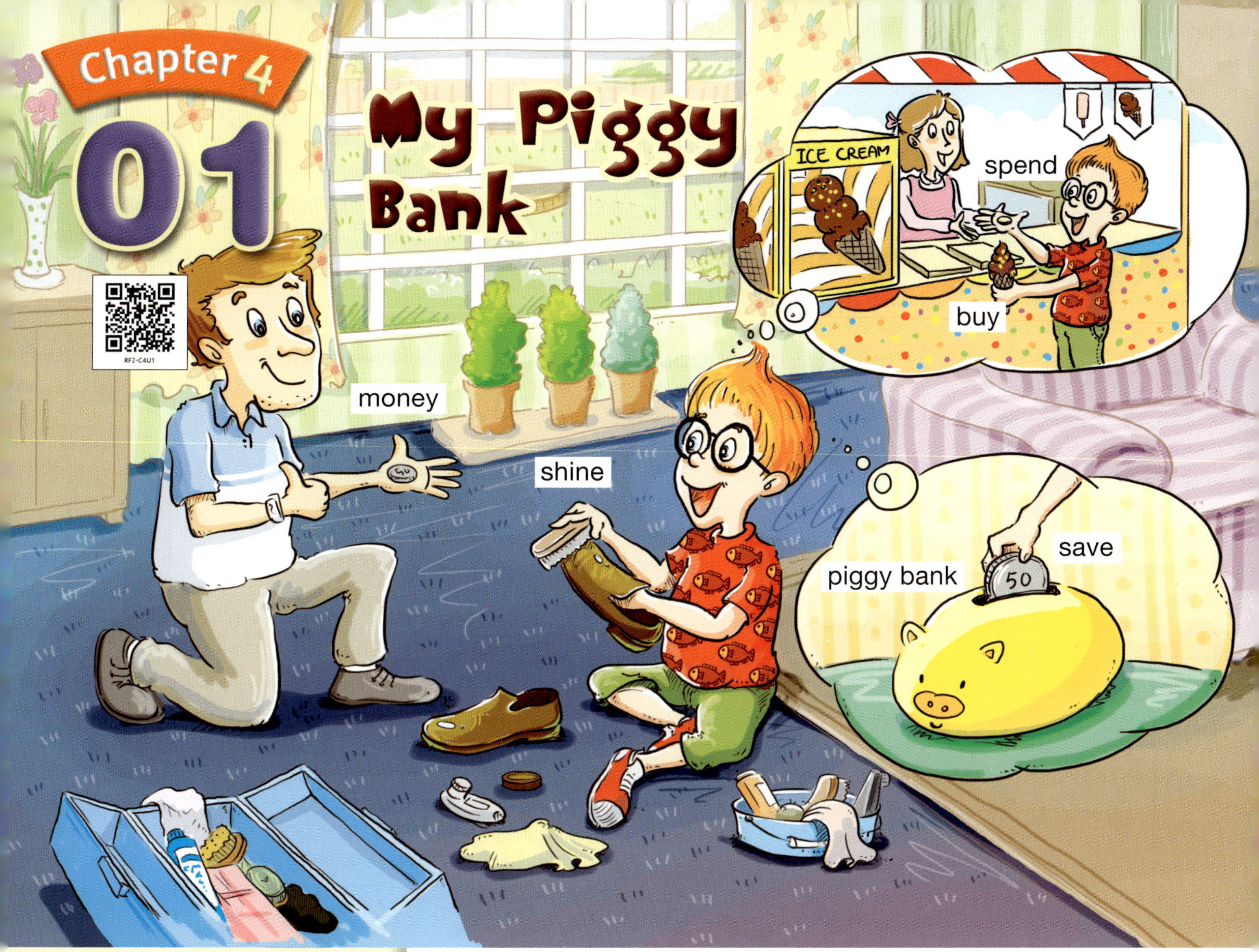

Get Ready

Look at the picture and talk about it.

1. What is the boy doing?
2. How much do you save a month?

Key Words

● Listen and write. MP3 02

1 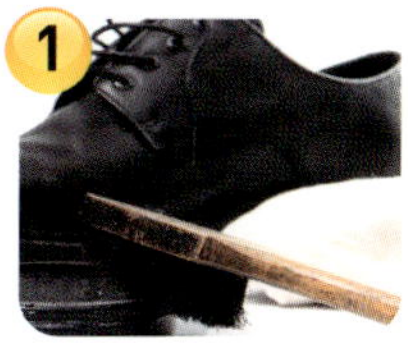

____

2

____

3

____

4

____

5

____

6

____

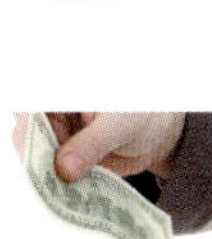

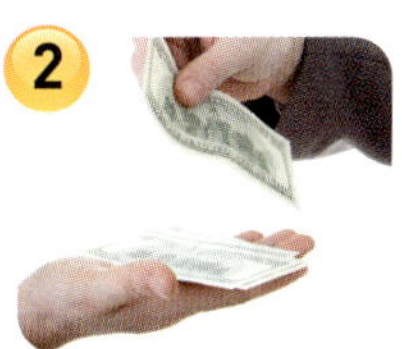

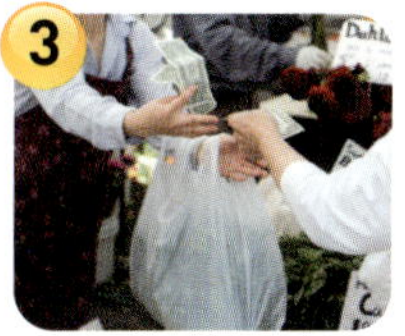

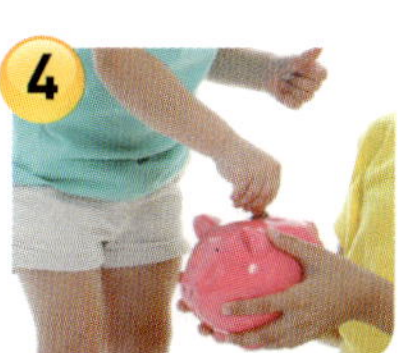

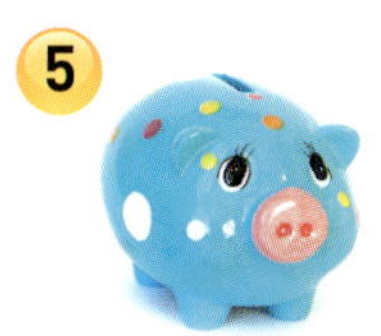

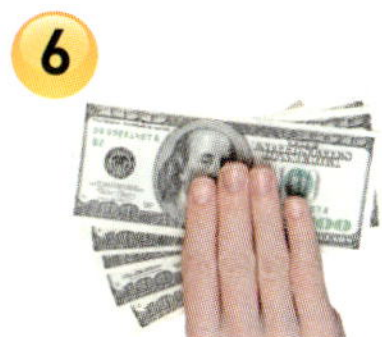

Jim washes dishes.

Mom gives him 70¢.

Jim shines dad's shoes.

Dad gives him 50¢.

Now, he can choose how to spend the money.

He can buy ice cream for 70¢.

He can buy chocolates for 50¢.

Or he can save the money for later.

Jim takes his piggy bank from the desk.

Ching! Ching!

He puts the money into the piggy bank.

"Next time, I'll have more money!"

Look!

- How many coins do you see in the picture?

→ There are __________ coins.

Check!

		True	False
1.	Jim makes 125¢ by helping his parents.	☐	☐
2.	Jim spends his money to buy ice cream.	☐	☐
3.	Jim wants to have more money in his piggy bank.	☐	☐

Reading Comprehension

● **Choose the best answer.**

1. What is the story about?
   a. getting money from parents
   b. spending money for food
   c. saving money with a piggy bank

2. Jim can choose how to ____________ his money.
   a. buy
   b. spend
   c. save

3. Jim can buy chocolates for ____________ .
   a. 50 ¢
   b. 70 ¢
   c. 120 ¢

4. What does Jim do with his money?

   a. 
   b. 
   c. 

Reading Skills   Story Map

● **Fill in the chart.**

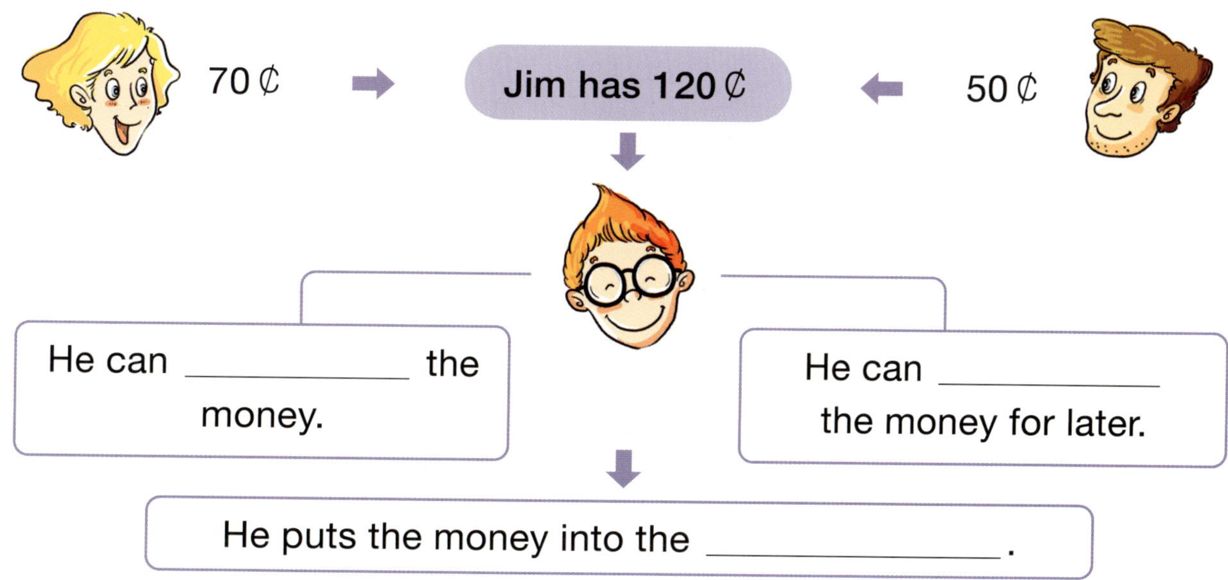

Word Challenge

- **Complete the word.**

1. 

sh□□e

2.

pi□□y bank

3.

m□n□y

- **Listen and write the correct word.** 📄 06

4. I need to _______________ money.

5. I want to _______________ some candies.

6. How much do you _______________ on food?

Your Turn

- **Look at the picture. Then ask and answer questions with your partner.**

Chapter 4

02 My Busy Mom!

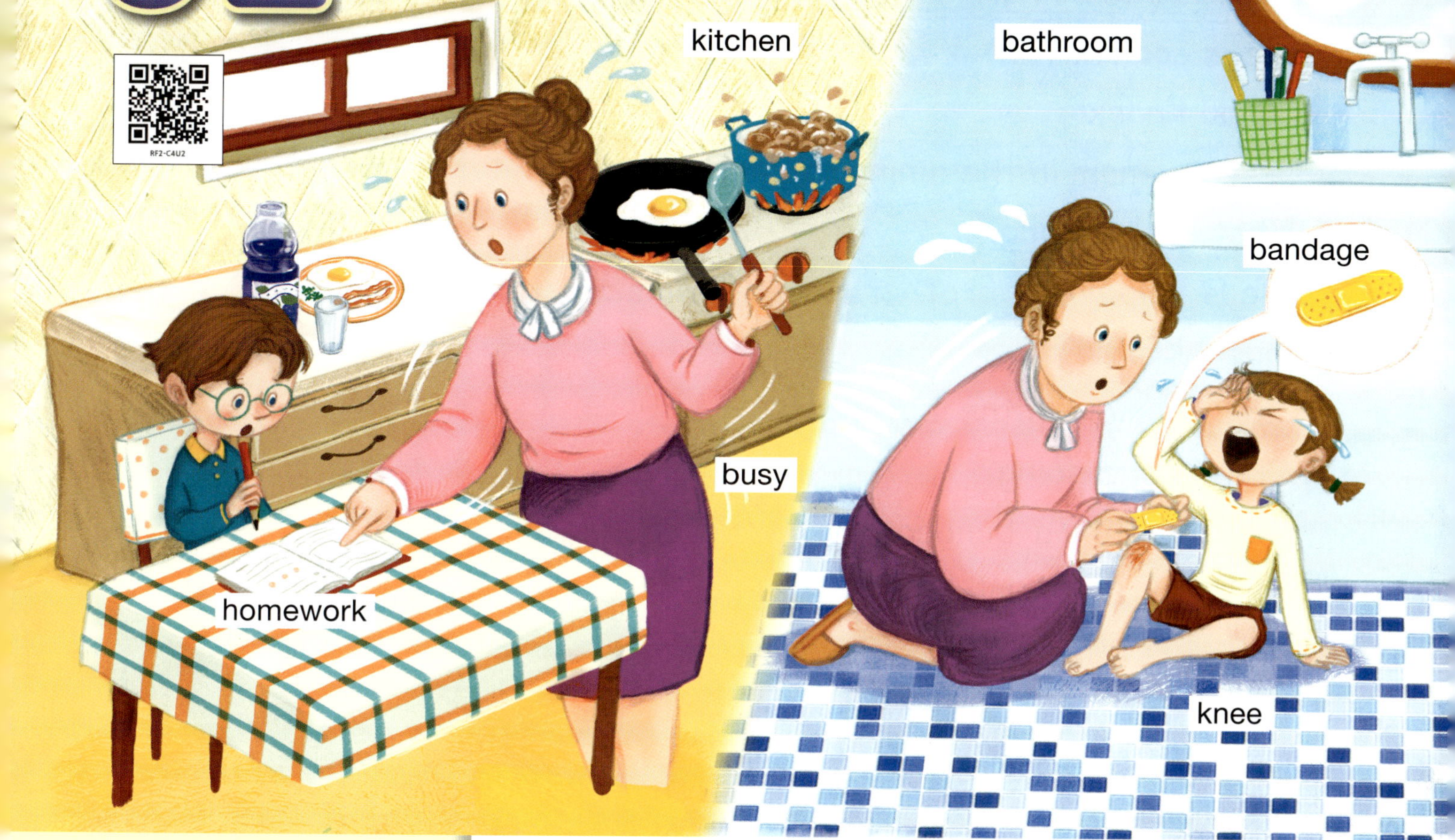

Get Ready

Look at the picture and talk about it.

1. What is the woman doing?
2. What kind of work does your mom do?

Key Words

Listen and write. MP3 07

1
______

2
______

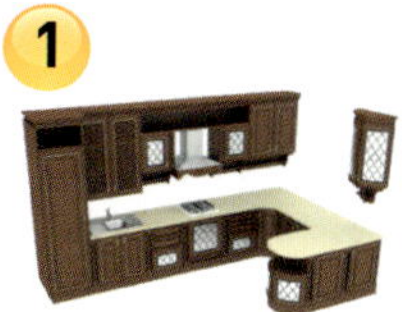

3
______

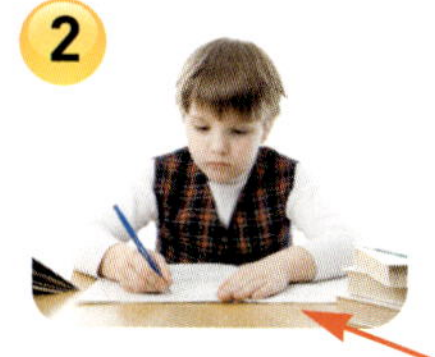

4
______

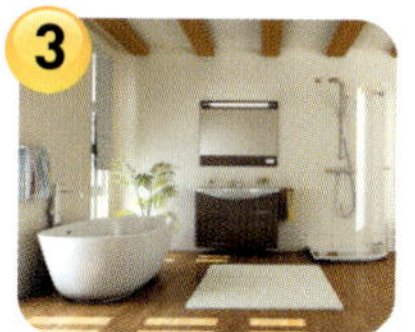

5
______

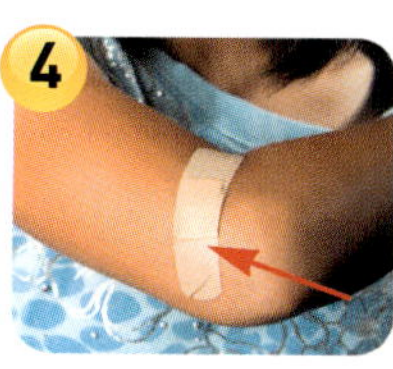

6
______

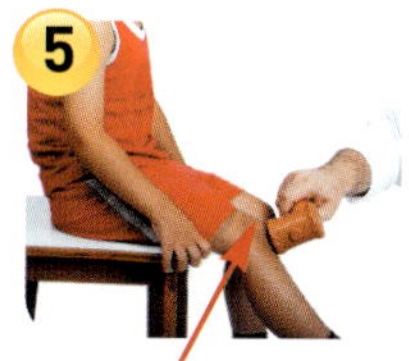

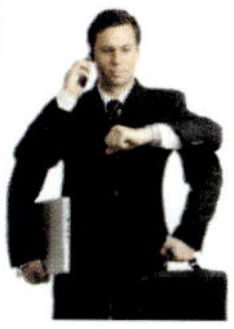

I see my mom in the kitchen.

What is she doing?

She is cooking.

Knock! Knock!

I see my mom in the dining room.

What is she doing?

She is helping my brother with his homework.

Knock! Knock!

I see my mom in the bathroom.

What is she doing?

She is putting a bandage on my sister's knee.

What a busy mom!

Look!

- Count the places where the boy's mom is in the picture.

→ She is in _________ different places.

Check!

1. The boy sees his mom outside the house.
2. The boy's mom is putting a bandage on her arm.
3. The boy's mom is busy.

Reading Comprehension

● **Choose the best answer.**

1. What is the story about?
   a. my busy mom
   b. my little brother and sister
   c different rooms at home

2. The boy's mom is ______________ in the kitchen.
   a. cooking   **b.** cleaning   **c.** serving

3. The boy's mom is helping his little brother with his ______________ .
   a. housework   **b.** homework   **c.** exercise

4. What is the boy's mom doing in the bathroom?

a.    **b.**    **c.** 

Reading Skills   Identifying Details

● **Fill in the chart.**

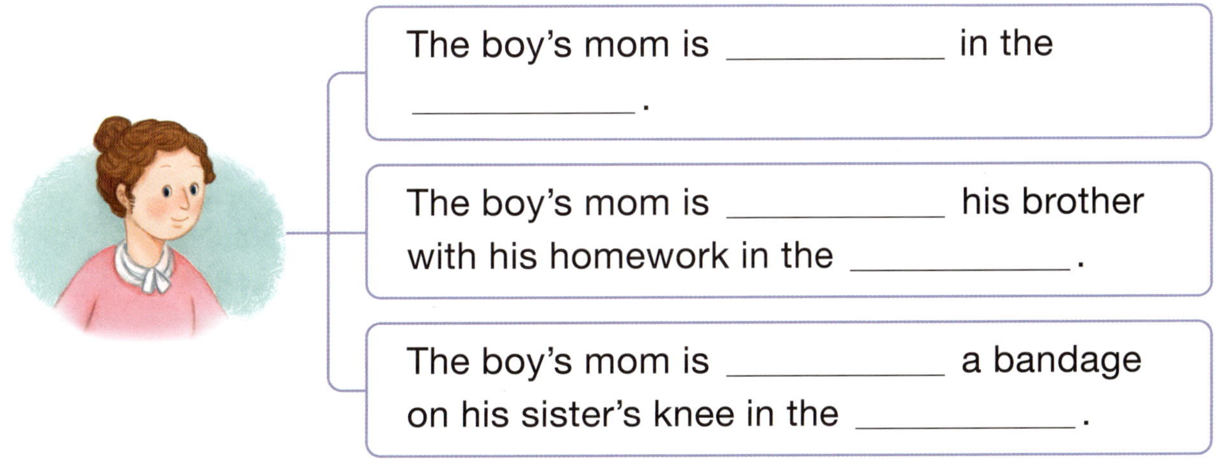

The boy's mom is ______________ in the ______________ .

The boy's mom is ______________ his brother with his homework in the ______________ .

The boy's mom is ______________ a bandage on his sister's knee in the ______________ .

Word Challenge

● Unscramble the word.

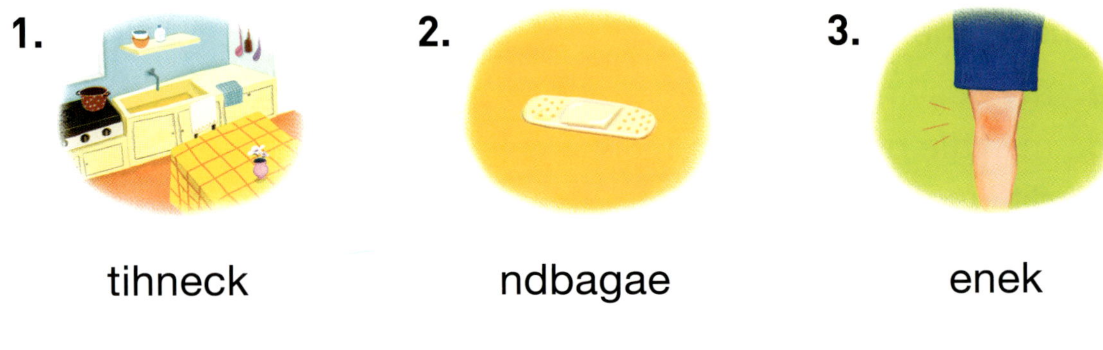

1. tihneck

2. ndbagae

3. enek

● Listen and circle the correct word. .MP3 11

4. We are (busy / happy) today.

5. You have to do your (best / homework).

6. They have two (bedrooms / bathrooms) in their house.

Your Turn

● Look at the picture of Rob's family. Then describe what each person is doing.

03 Interview with a Farmer

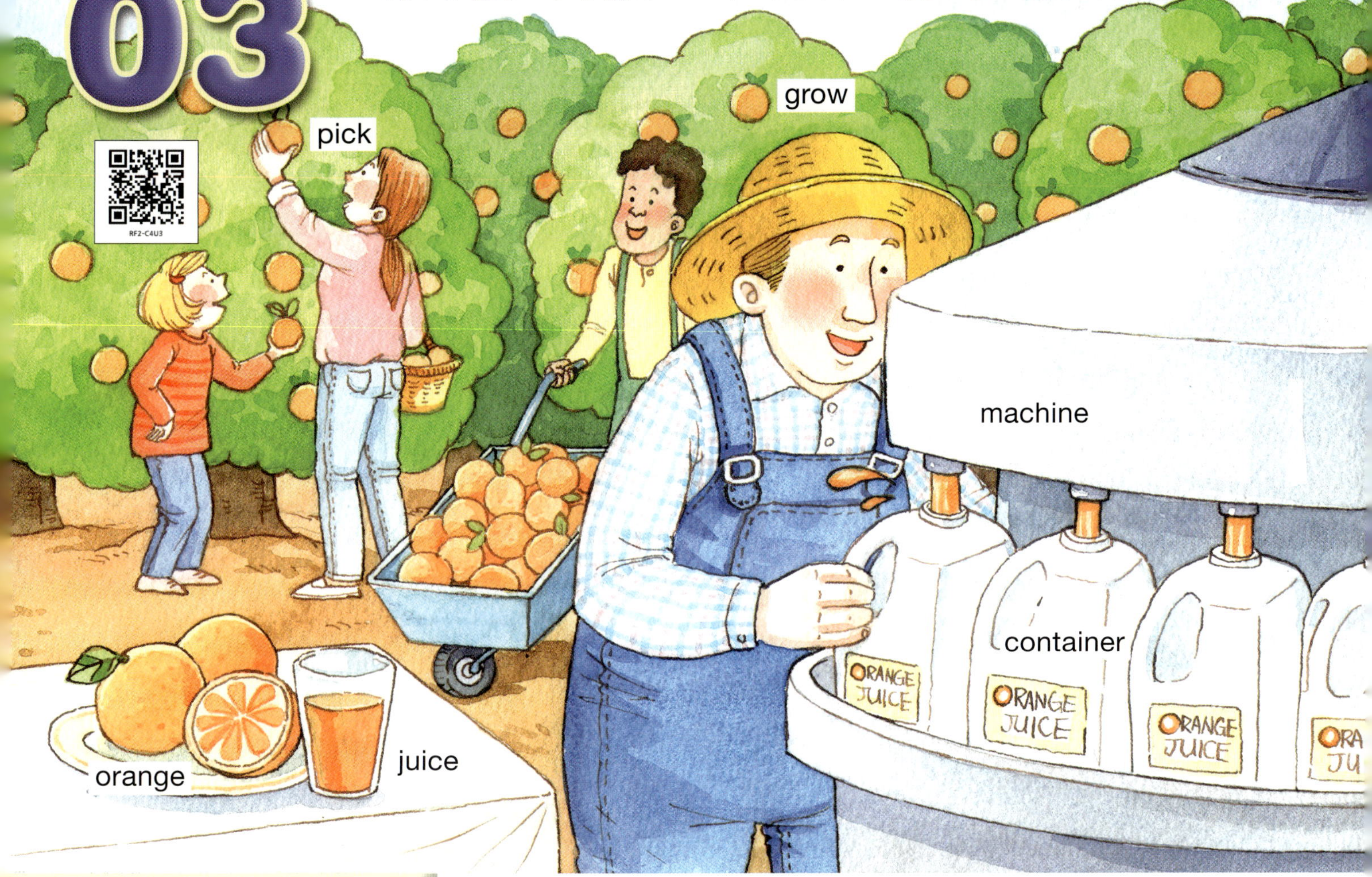

Get Ready

Look at the picture and talk about it.

1. Where are they?

2. How do we get orange juice from orange trees?

Key Words

● Listen and write. 🎵12

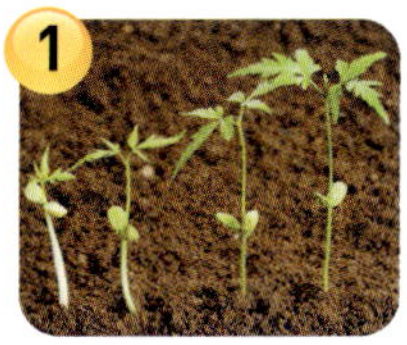

What do you do?

I **grow** **orange** trees.

I love orange **juice**.

How do we get orange juice from your trees?

It takes a lot of work.

First, we **pick** the oranges.

Next, we move them to the squeezing **machine**.

Then, we put the juice into **containers**.

It's a lot of work!

Later, the juice containers are sent to the stores.

Then, we can buy them there.

Thanks, Mr. Frank!

Look!

- What is the boy doing in the picture?

→ He is ___________ with a farmer.

Check!

	True	False
1. Mr. Frank is a farmer.	☐	☐
2. The boy loves tomato juice.	☐	☐
3. It's little work to get orange juice from orange trees.	☐	☐

Reading Comprehension

● **Choose the best answer.**

1. What is the story about?
- **a.** growing orange trees
- **b.** picking oranges from trees
- **c.** getting orange juice from orange trees

2. It ____________ a lot of work to get orange juice from orange trees.

a. makes   **b.** takes   **c.** spends

3. The boy can ____________ orange juice at the stores.

a. sell   **b.** buy   **c.** send

4. What does Mr. Frank do?

a.    **b.**    **c.** 

Reading Skills   Sequencing

● **Fill in the chart.**

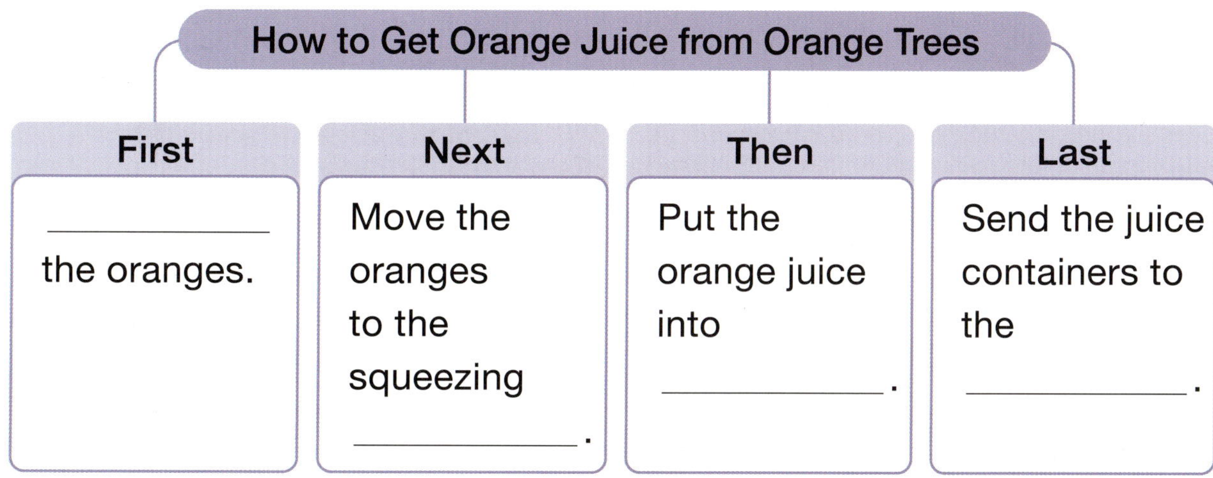

Word Challenge

- Check the correct word for each picture.

1. 

☐ kick
☐ pick

2. 

☐ range
☐ orange

3. 

☐ grow
☐ throw

- Listen and put an **X** on the wrong word. Write the correct word. 🎧 16

4. I like to drink milk. _______________

5. Put your cups in the box. _______________

6. The man is fixing the car. _______________

Your Turn

- Draw your favorite person. Then complete the questions and answers.

1. Who is your favorite person?   His / Her name is ____________ .

2. __________ does he / she do?   He / She is a(n) ____________ .

3. __________ old is he / she?   He / She is ____________ years old.

4. __________ does he / she live?   He / She lives in ____________ .

Chapter 4

04 Why do People Work?

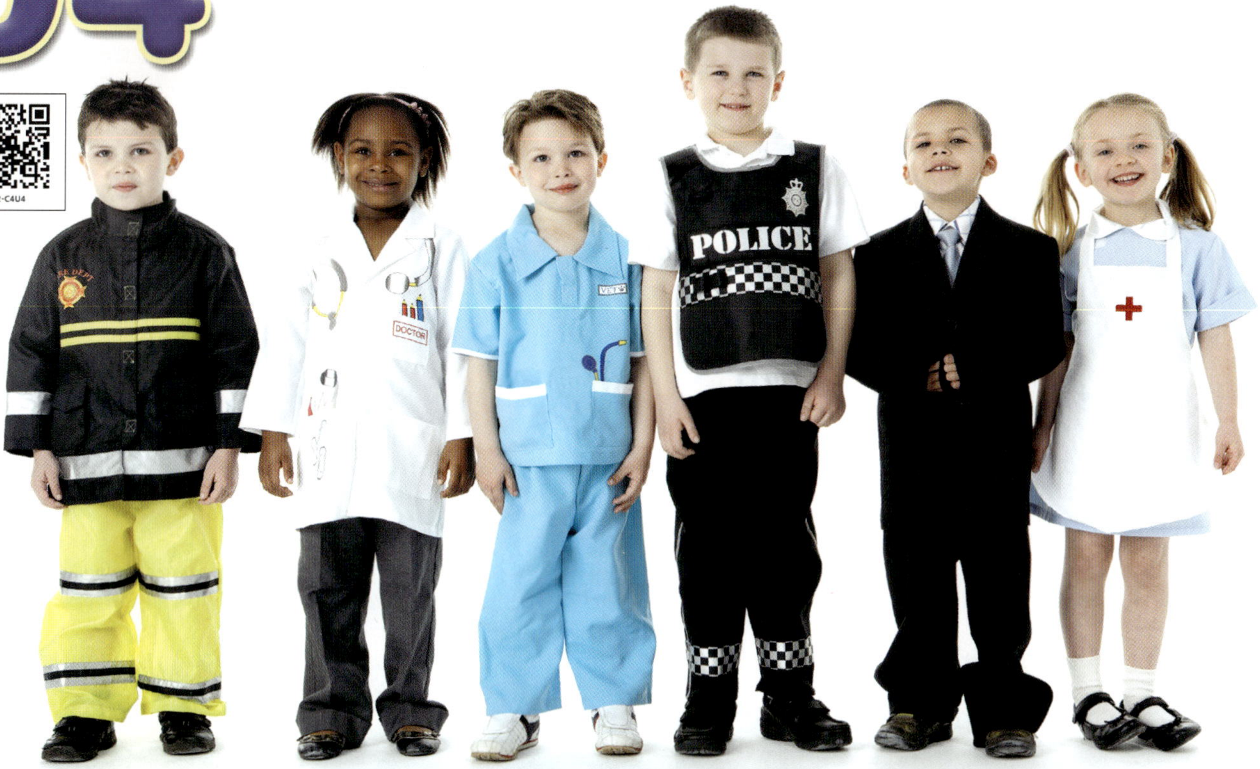

Get Ready

Look at the picture and talk about it.

1. What kind of jobs do you see in the picture?
2. Why do you think people work?

Key Words

Listen and write. MP3 17

earn goods pay telephone clerk job

1 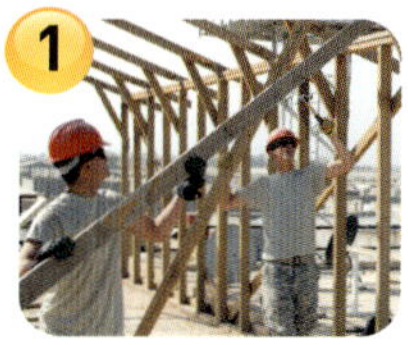 ____________

2 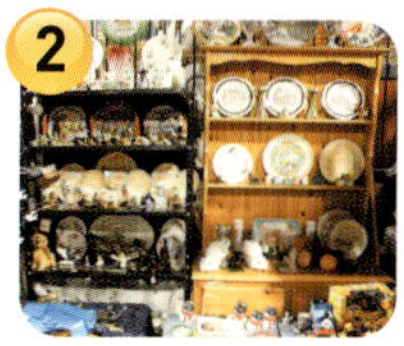 ____________

3 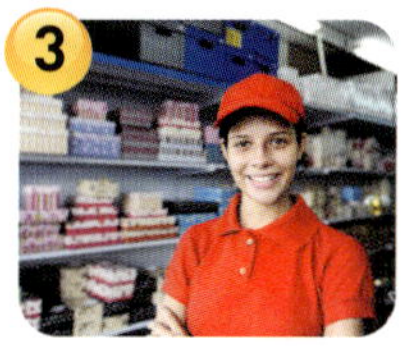 ____________

4 ____________

5 ____________

6 ____________

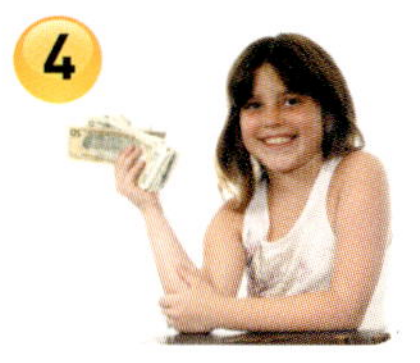

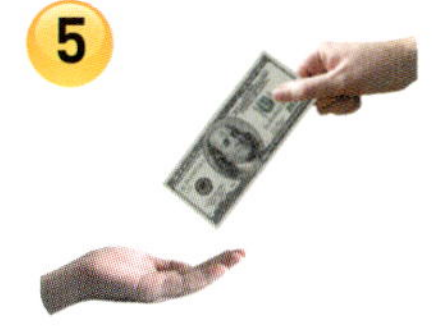

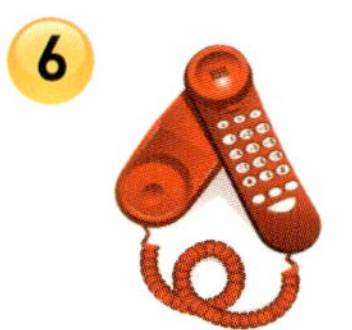

Most people have jobs.

Some people work inside.

Some work outside.

Why do people work?

They work to get goods.

They work to get services.

Mr. Brian works as a clerk.

He earns money for his work.

What does he do with his money?

He buys goods like food and clothes.

He pays for using services like a bus
and a telephone.

What other goods and services can he get?

Look!

- How many people are in the pictures?
- → There are _______ people.

Check!

	True	False
1. Most people work.	☐	☐
2. Some people work outside.	☐	☐
3. We spend money for goods and services.	☐	☐

Reading Comprehension

● **Choose the best answer.**

1. What is the story about?
- **a.** why people work
- **b.** different kinds of jobs
- **c.** how people make money

2. People work to get goods and ____________ .
- **a.** clothing
- **b.** telephone
- **c.** services

3. Mr. Brian ____________ money for his work.
- **a.** earns
- **b.** buys
- **c.** pays

4. What does Mr. Brian do?

a. 　　**b.** 　　**c.** 

Reading Skills Identifying Reasons

● **Fill in the chart.**

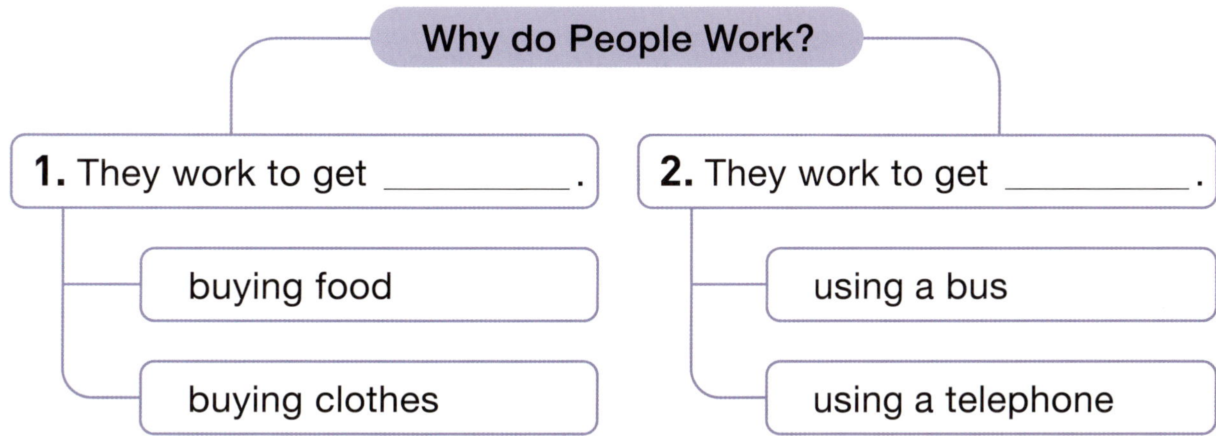

Word Challenge

● **Cross out the unrelated word.**

1. job   nurse   robber   teacher
2. goods   milk   help   television
3. service   bank   hospital   farm

● **Listen and write the correct word.** MP3 21

4. I can't use this ________________ .

5. She should ________________ for her food.

6. The ________________ at the shop is very kind.

Your Turn

● **Draw goods and services that you use every day. Then talk about how they help you.**

Chapter 5

01 MOTHER NATURE'S HOLIDAYS

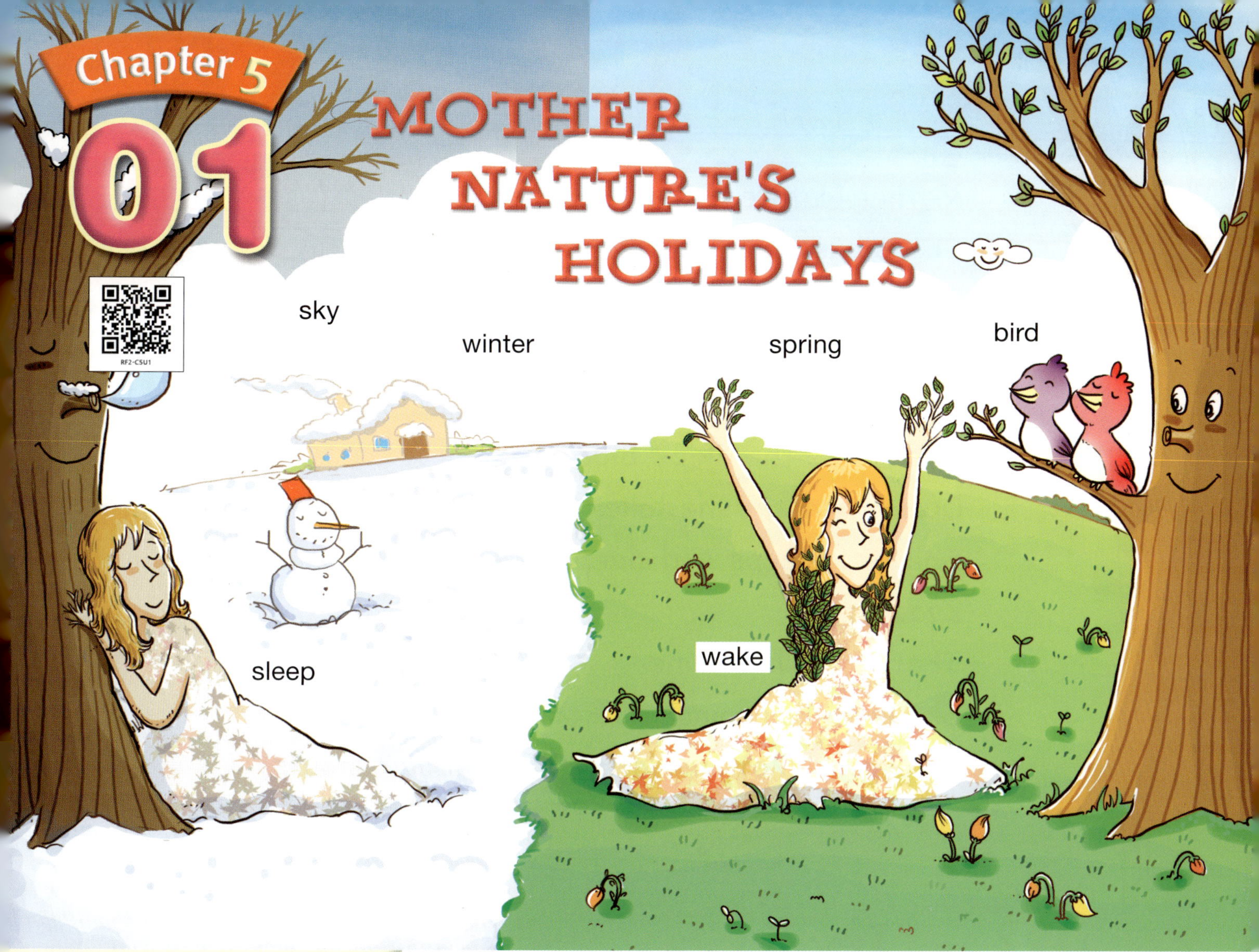

Get Ready

Look at the picture and talk about it.

1. What is Mother Nature doing in the winter scene?
2. What do you see in the spring scene?

Key Words

- Listen and write. MP3 22

1 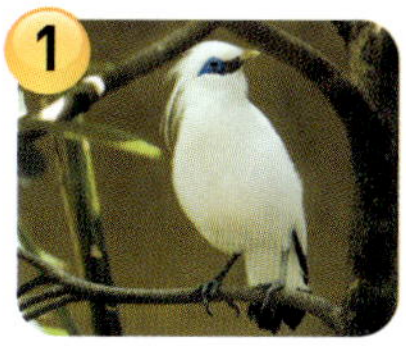
______

2
______

3
______

4
______

5
______

6
______

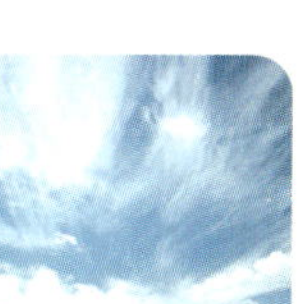

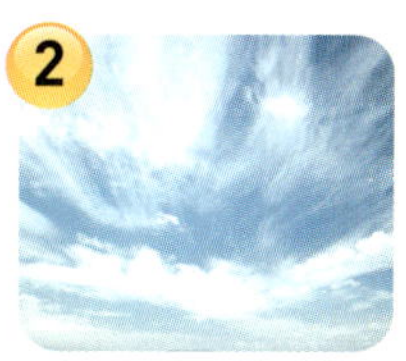

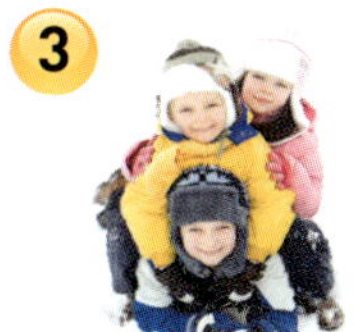

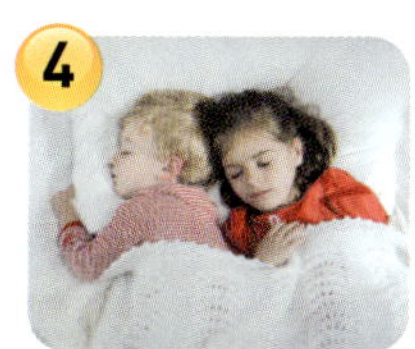

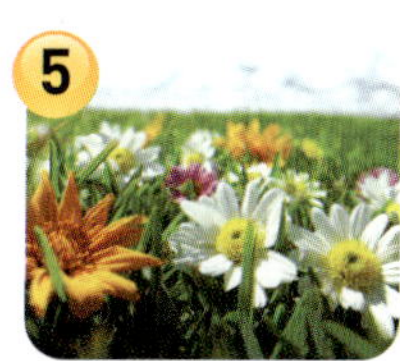

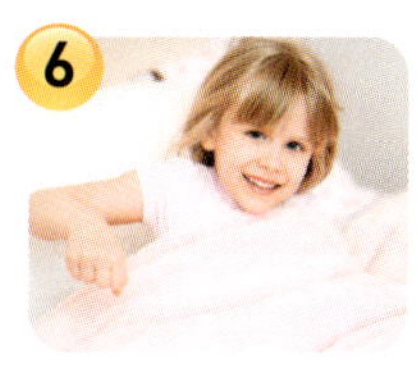

Look!

- Count the number of trees, clouds, and birds and add them together.

→ It's __________ .

Check!

	True	False
1. Mother Nature works hard every season.	☐	☐
2. Mother Nature makes the skies blue in spring.	☐	☐
3. Mother Nature doesn't sleep at all.	☐	☐

Reading Comprehension

● **Choose the best answer.**

1. What is the story about?
   a. winter and spring
   b. Mother Nature's friends in spring
   c. Mother Nature's long break in winter

2. Mother Nature is ____________ every spring.
   a. free   b. busy   c. sleepy

3. Mother Nature ____________ in winter.
   a. works   b. dreams   c. sleeps

4. What does Mother Nature not do in spring?

a.    b.    c. 

Reading Skills   Compare and Contrast

● **Fill in the chart.**

It is ____________ .

Mother Nature ____________ .

It is ____________ .

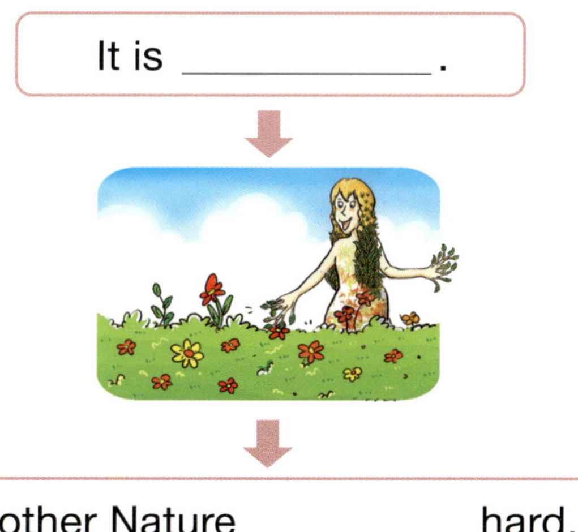

Mother Nature ____________ hard.

Word Challenge

● **Complete the word.**

1. 

s☐☐

2. 

sl☐☐p

3. 

wi☐☐er

● **Listen and write the correct word.** MP3 26

4. I usually _______________ up at 7.

5. The _______________ is on the fence.

6. The sun is bright in _______________ .

Your Turn

● **Look at the picture. Then describe how each person spends his or her holiday.**

Chapter 5

02 Spring Rain

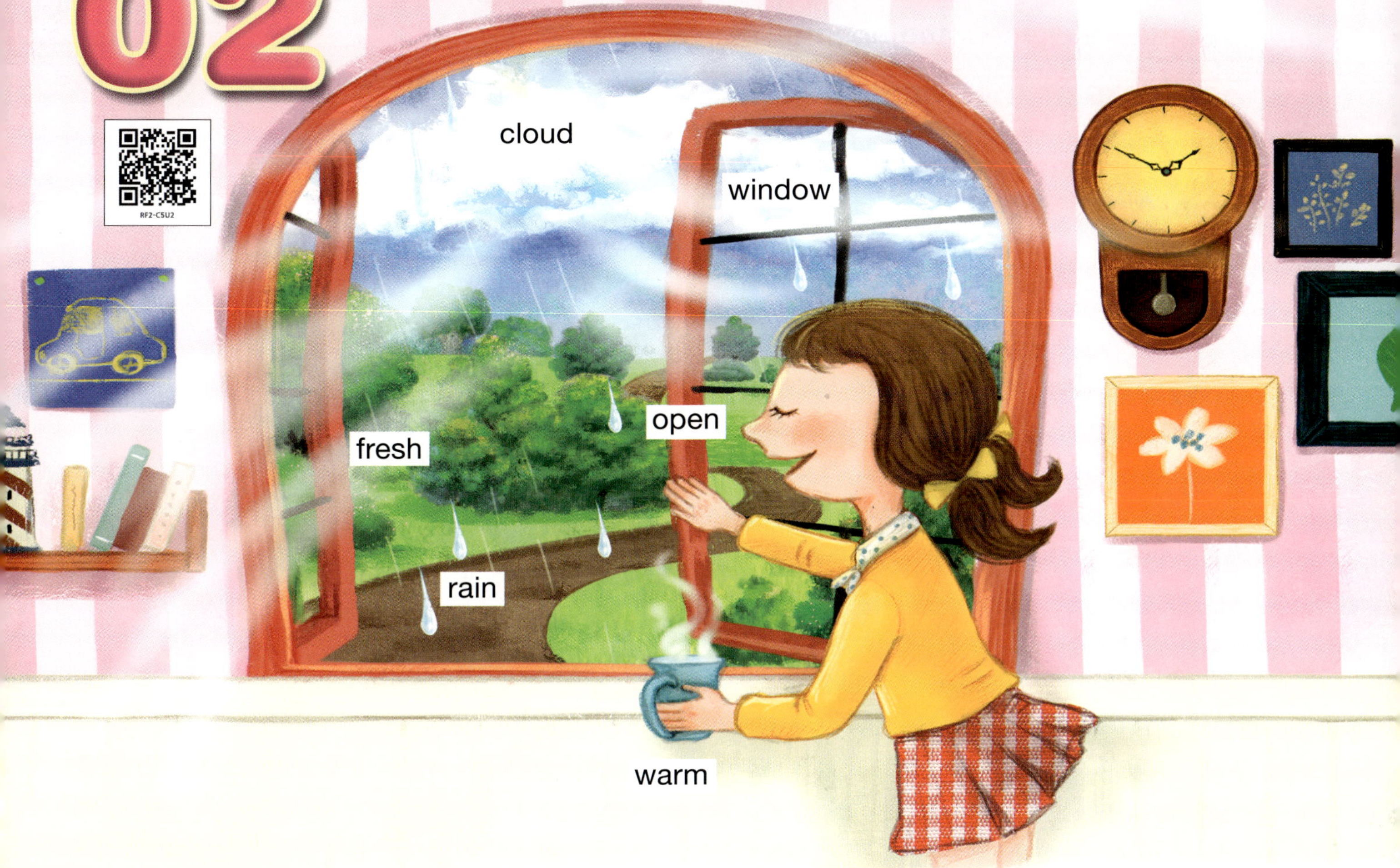

Get Ready

Look at the picture and talk about it.

1. What is the girl doing?
2. How do you know when spring has come?

Key Words

Listen and write. MP3 27

1 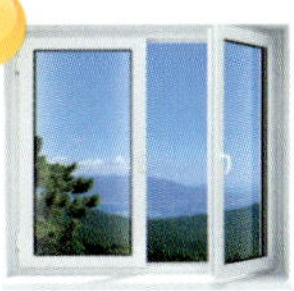
______

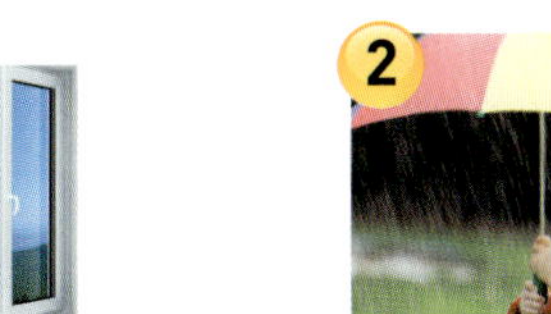

2
______

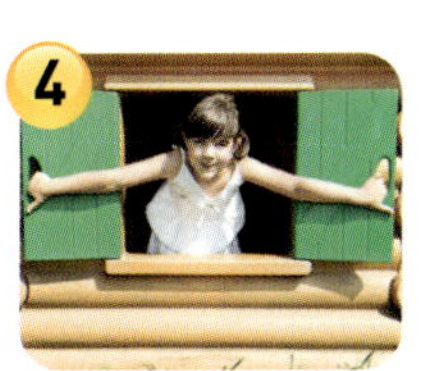

3
______

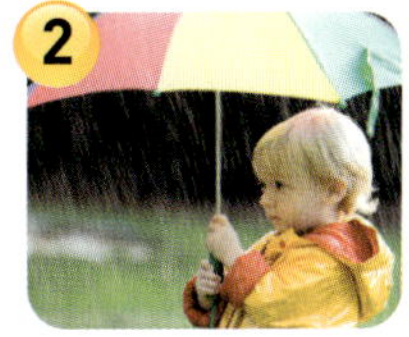

4
______

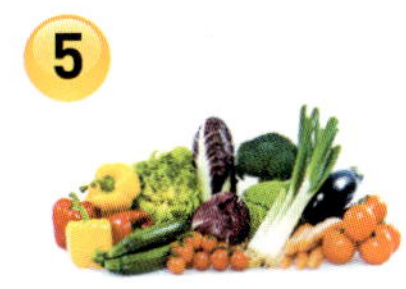

5
______

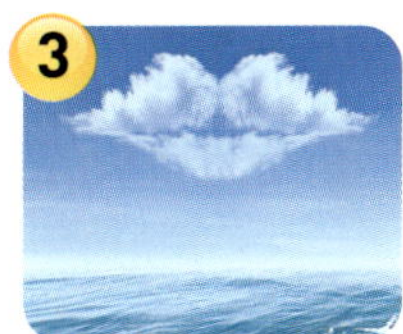

6
______

Look!

- What insect do you see in the picture?

→ I see a __________ .

Check!

	True	False
1. Judy hears some breaking sounds.	☐	☐
2. Some fresh air blows in Judy's face.	☐	☐
3. Judy thinks spring has come.	☐	☐

Reading Comprehension

● **Choose the best answer.**

1. What is the story about?
   a. some tapping sounds
   b. feeling spring in the air
   c. moving clouds in the sky

2. What is hitting the window?
   a. rain   b. snow   c. wind

3. What does Judy feel?
   a. hot air   b. warm air   c. cold air

4. What does Judy see in the sky?

   a.    b.    c. 

Reading Skills   Cause and Effect

● **Fill in the chart.**

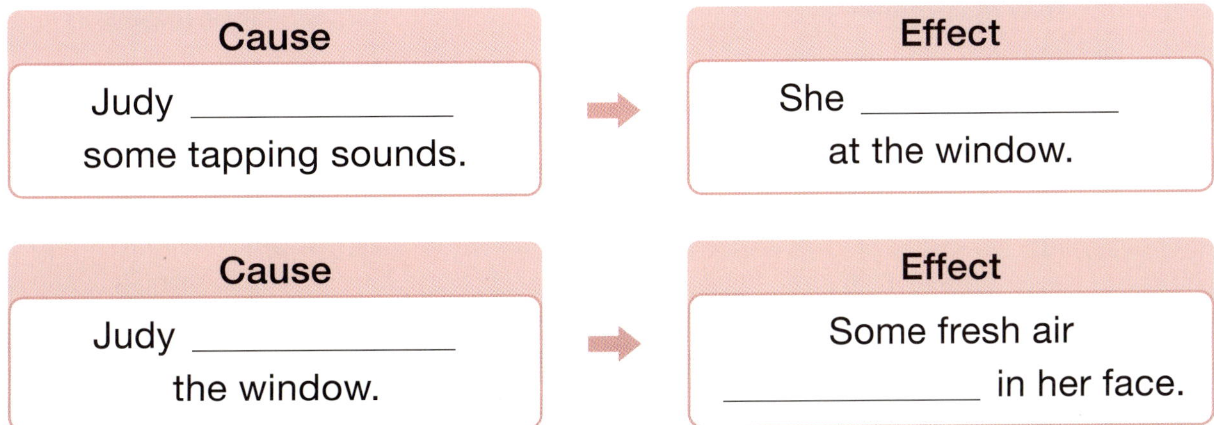

Cause		Effect
Judy ______________ some tapping sounds.	→	She ______________ at the window.
Judy ______________ the window.	→	Some fresh air ______________ in her face.

Word Challenge

- Unscramble the word.

1. nira

2. pnoe

3. cudol

- Listen and circle the correct word. 31

4. It's (warm / hot) in here.

5. The TV is next to the (door / window).

6. I want to breathe (cool / fresh) air.

Your Turn

- Draw the missing picture and tell the story.

Chapter 5

03 Clothes and Activities for the Season

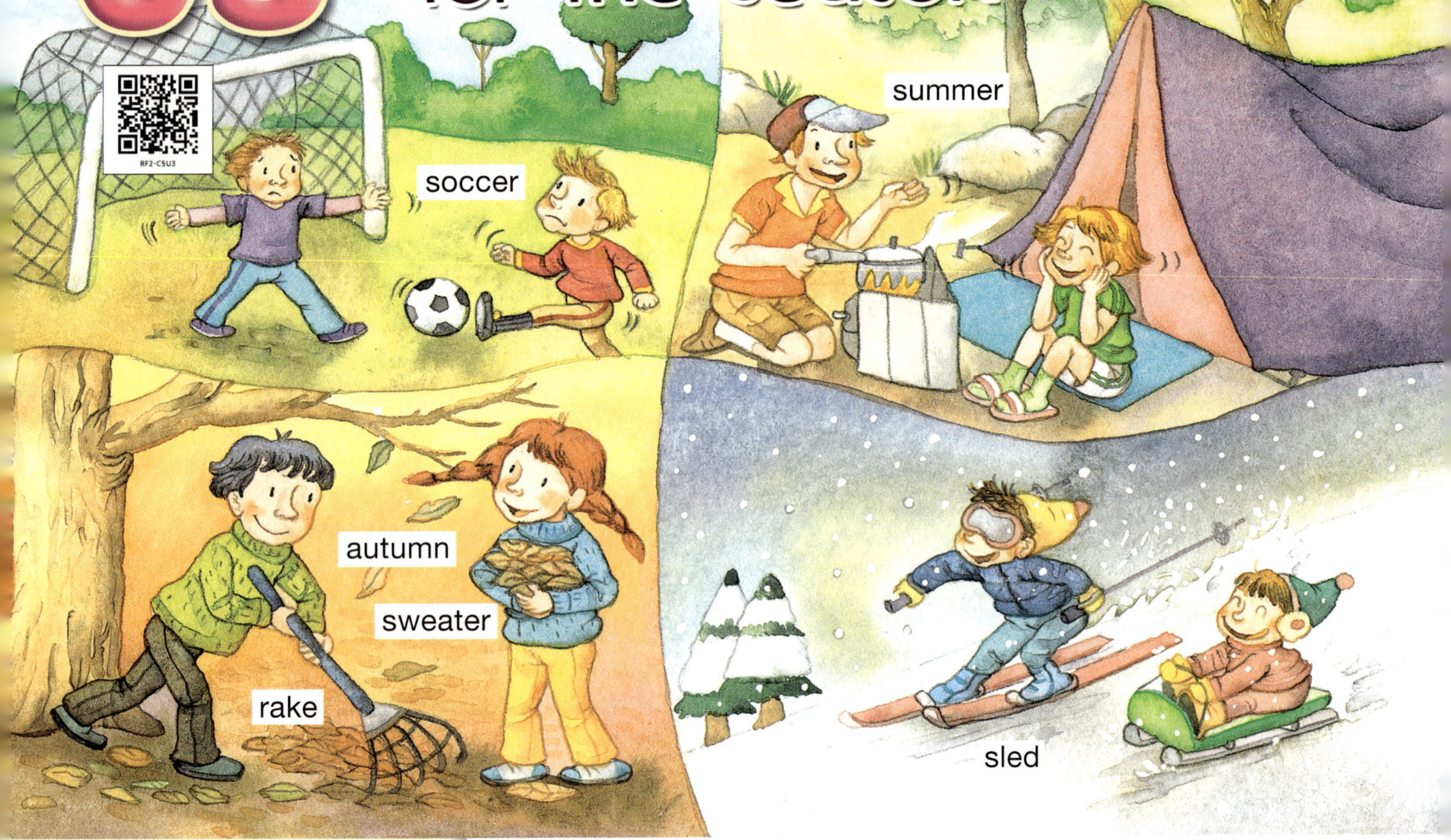

Get Ready

Look at the picture and talk about it.

1. What are they doing in the summer scene?
2. What do you wear in each season?

Key Words

Listen and write. MP3 32

1 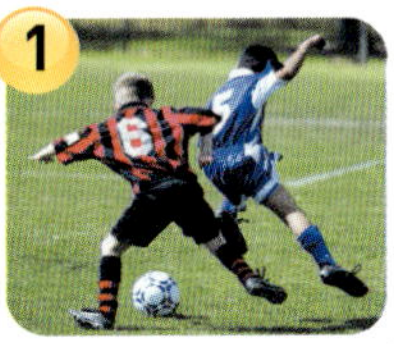
______

2
______

3
______

4
______

5
______

6
______

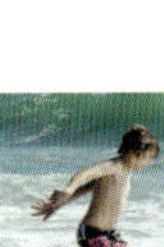

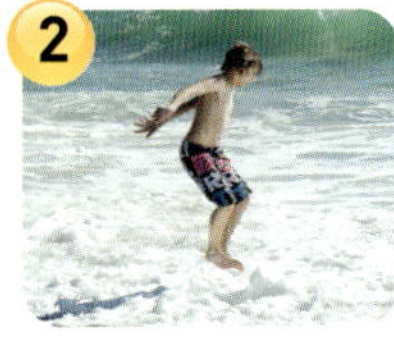

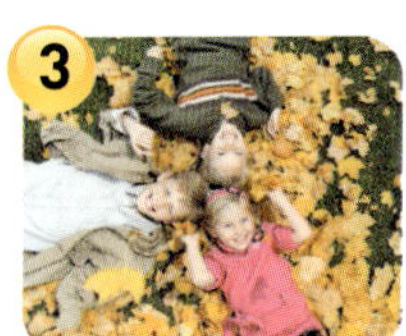

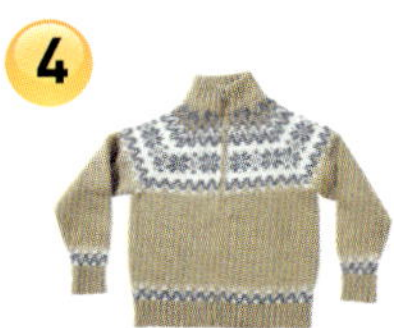

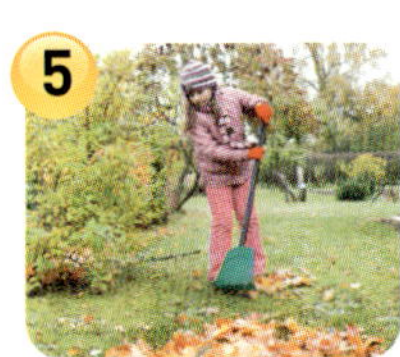

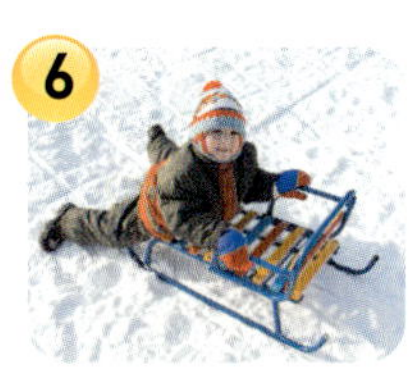

Seasons change what people wear.
Seasons change what people do.
In spring, people wear light jackets.
They like to play baseball and soccer.
In summer, people wear shorts and sandals.
Families go fishing and camping.
In autumn, people get ready for winter.
They wear long pants and sweaters.
They rake leaves on the street.
People dress warmly in winter.
They wear coats and boots.
Children go sledding and skiing.

Look!

- How many people do you see in the winter scene?
- → There are _________ people.

Check!

		True	False
1. Seasons change what people wear.		☐	☐
2. People wear light jackets in spring.		☐	☐
3. Families go fishing and camping in summer.		☐	☐

Reading Comprehension

● **Choose the best answer.**

1. What is the story about?
   a. different clothes for the season
   b. different activities for the season
   c. different clothes and activities for the season

2. People wear ______________ and sandals in summer.
   a. shorts
   b. sweaters
   c. coats

3. When do people rake leaves on the street?
   a. spring
   b. summer
   c. autumn

4. What do people do in winter?

a. 
b. 
c. 

Reading Skills   Classifying

● **Fill in the chart.**

Season	What People Wear	What People Do
Spring	light ____________	baseball and ____________
Summer	shorts and ____________	____________ and camping
Autumn	long pants and ____________	raking ____________
Winter	____________ and boots	____________ and skiing

Word Challenge

● **Check the correct word for each picture.**

1.

- [ ] bake
- [ ] rake

2.

- [ ] glad
- [ ] sled

3.

- [ ] drummer
- [ ] summer

● **Listen and put an X on the wrong word. Write the correct word.** 🎵 36

4. I like winter in Korea. ________________

5. Do you have a red coat? ________________

6. They are playing baseball. ________________

Your Turn

● **Check when you do each activity and talk about it.**

04 Saving Water

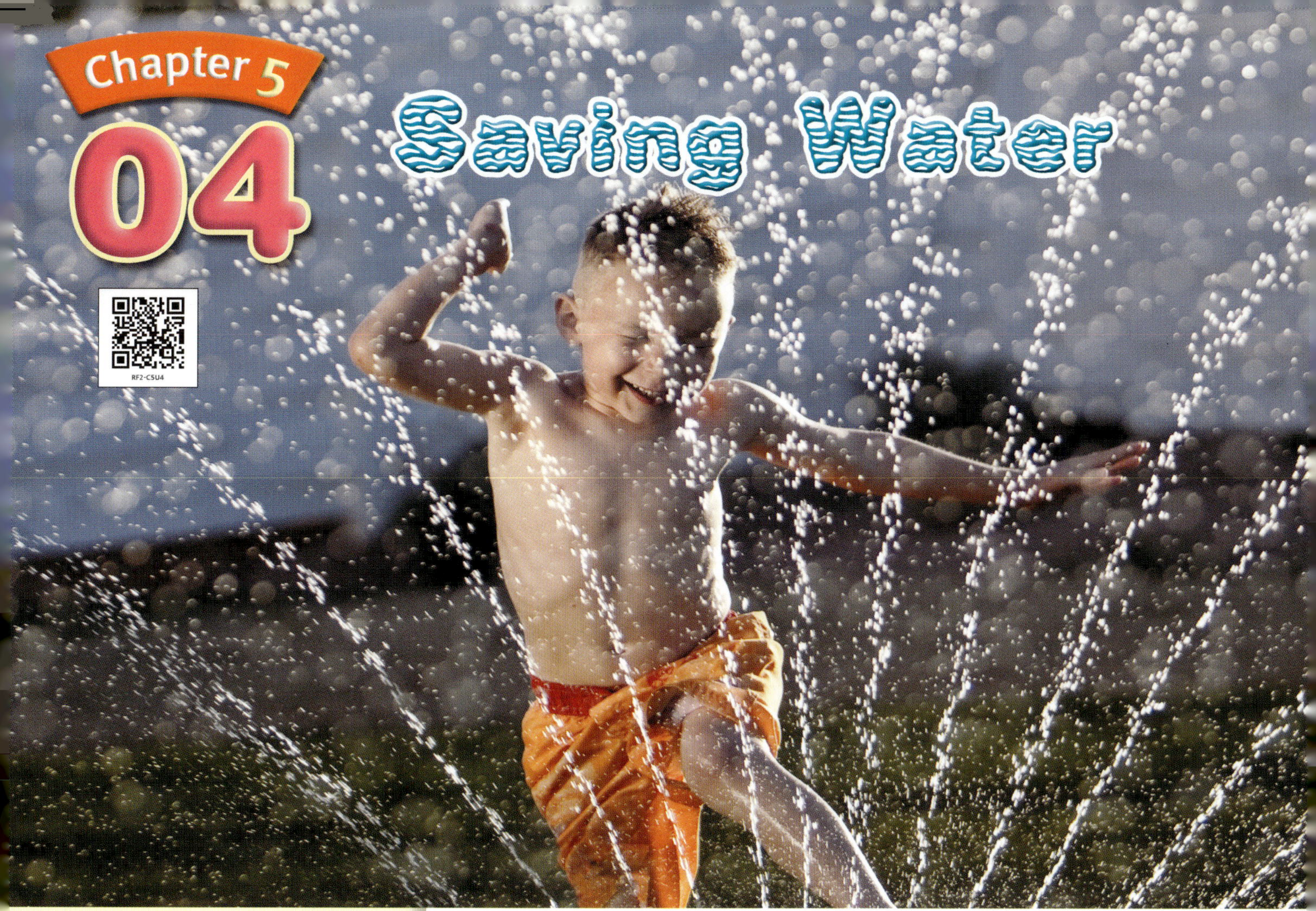

Get Ready

Look at the picture and talk about it.

1. What is the boy doing?

2. How can we save water at home?

Key Words

● Listen and write. [MP3] 37

cook   flush   faucet   earth   shower   drink

We use water every day.

We use water for bathing.

We use water for drinking and cooking.

We need water to live.

But we don't have enough water on earth.

How can you save water?

Here are things you can do at home.

Take short showers.

Turn off the faucet when brushing your teeth.

Don't change your clothes too often.

Don't flush the toilet too often.

We need to work together to save water.

Look!

- How many children do you see in the pictures?
→ There are ___________ children.

Check!

	True	False
1. We use water every day.	☐	☐
2. We need water to live.	☐	☐
3. We should not change our clothes very often.	☐	☐

Reading Comprehension

● **Choose the best answer.**

1. What is the story about?
- **a.** sources of water
- **b.** why we need water
- **c.** how we save water at home

2. We use water for _____________ .
- **a.** sleeping
- **b.** cooking
- **c.** reading

3. We need to take _____________ showers to save water.
- **a.** short
- **b.** long
- **c.** cold

4. What can we do to save water at home?

a.  **b.**  **c.** 

Reading Skills   Drawing Conclusions

● **Fill in the chart.**

We need _________________ to live.

We don't have _________________ water on earth.

We need to work together to _________________ water.

Word Challenge

● **Match each word with its meaning.**

1. cook   •   • prepare food for eating

2. drink   •   • clean a toilet with water

3. flush   •   • take liquid into your mouth and swallow it

● **Listen and write the correct word.** MP3 41

4. The _____________ is round.

5. I turn on the kitchen _____________.

6. She is taking a short _____________.

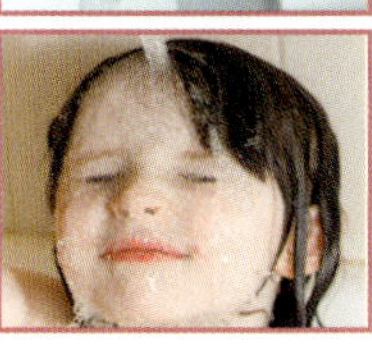

Your Turn

● **Check your daily habit of using water.**

Check List

	Yes	No
1. I take short showers.	☐	☐
2. I turn off the water when I brush my teeth.	☐	☐
3. I don't use a washing machine with a few items.	☐	☐
4. I don't flush too often.	☐	☐

Word List

Chapter 1	Chapter 2	Chapter 3
Unit 1	**Unit 1**	**Unit 1**
daydream	birthday	garden
ship	living room	plant
pirate	skirt	seed
bully	favorite	soil
afraid	move	sprout
shoot	dress	water
Unit 2	**Unit 2**	**Unit 2**
woods	baseball	apple
bear	pitcher	stretch
climb	throw	tall
ground	hit	wind
scared	bat	sweet
close	glove	delicious
Unit 3	**Unit 3**	**Unit 3**
different	concert	age
hear	manner	trunk
word	late	tree
talk	food	wide
spell	eat	narrow
question	picture	ring
Unit 4	**Unit 4**	**Unit 4**
fun	step	root
help	clap	stem
cheer	stamp	leaf
feel	feet	light
sad	spin	air
laugh	music	flower

Chapter 4	**Chapter 5**

Chapter 4

Unit 1
shine
spend
buy
save
piggy bank
money

Unit 2
kitchen
homework
bathroom
bandage
knee
busy

Unit 3
grow
orange
juice
pick
machine
container

Unit 4
job
goods
clerk
earn
pay
telephone

Chapter 5

Unit 1
bird
sky
winter
sleep
spring
wake

Unit 2
window
rain
cloud
open
fresh
warm

Unit 3
soccer
summer
autumn
sweater
rake
sled

Unit 4
drink
cook
earth
shower
faucet
flush

Reading
First
2
Workbook
WorldCom Edu

Reading First 2

Workbook

WorldCom Edu

01 Joe's Daydream

Word Practice

- Write the correct word for each picture. Then circle 6 words in the box.

1. ___________________

2. ___________________

3. ___________________

4. ___________________

5. ___________________

6. ___________________

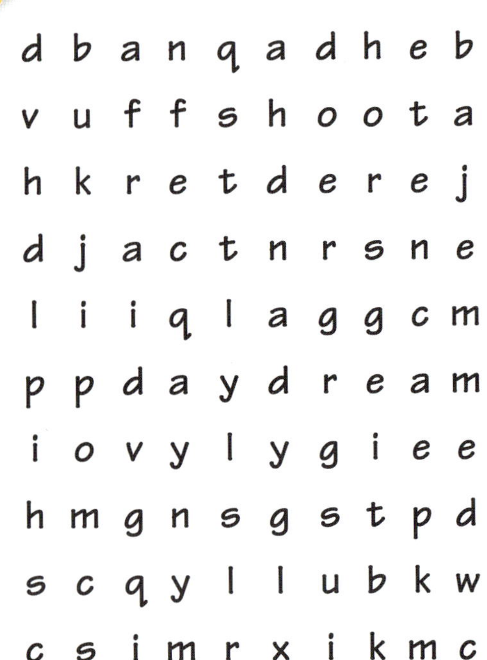

- Choose the correct word for each sentence.

in	book	land

1. He is ___________ the living room.

2. There is a ___________ on the desk.

3. We fall and ___________ on the ground.

Sentence Practice

- Unscramble the sentences.

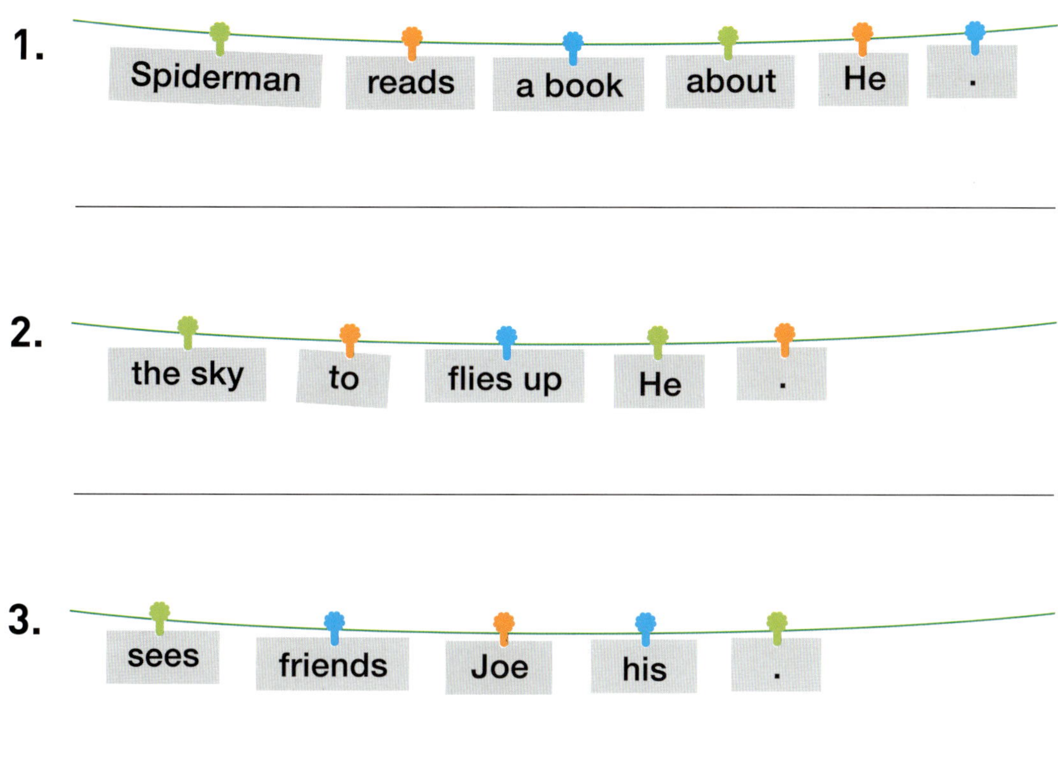

1.

____

2.

____

3.

____

- Read the passage of the unit and match the sentence parts.

1. Joe is   •   • bullying his friends.

2. The pirates are   •   • his spider-webs.

3. He shoots   •   • Spiderman.

4. He saves   •   • his friends.

02 True Friend?

Word Practice

- Complete the crossword puzzle.

- Choose the correct word for each sentence.

lie	choose	carefully

1. You need to think ____________ .

2. Do not ____________ down here.

3. You can ____________ your team leader.

Sentence Practice

- Unscramble the sentences.

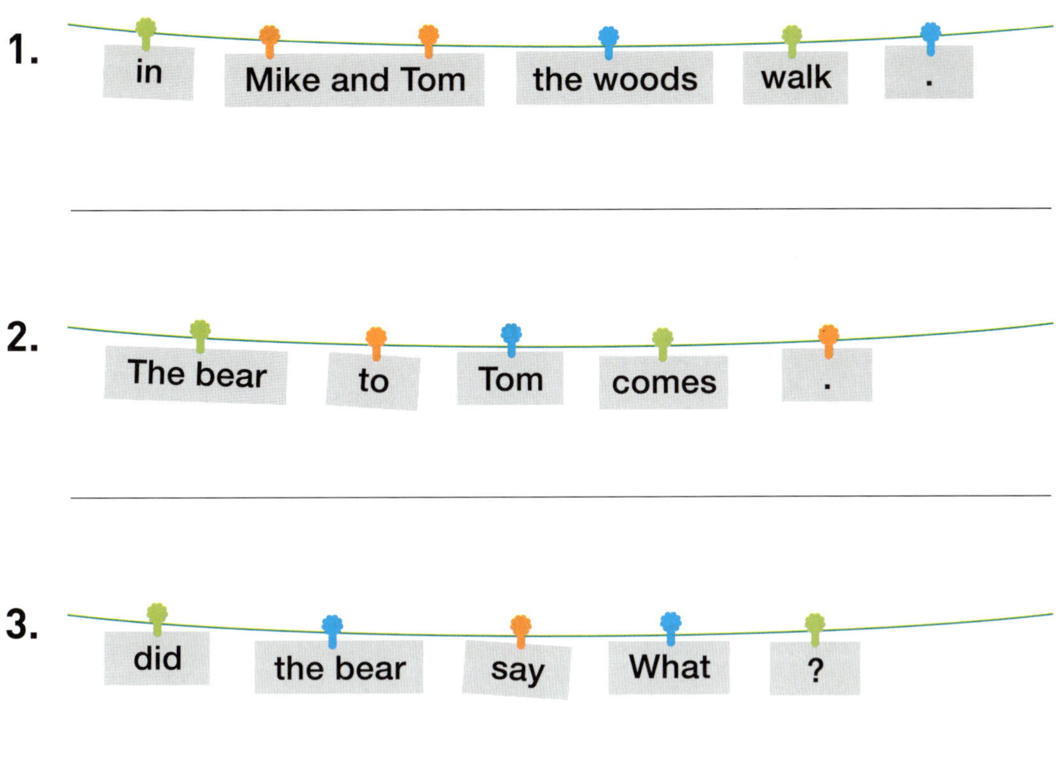

____

- Read the passage of the unit and match the sentence parts.

1. Suddenly, a bear   •   • 'Choose your friend carefully!'

2. Mike alone   •   • on the ground.

3. Tom lies   •   • climbs up a tree.

4. The bear said,   •   • shows up.

03 Molly's Friend, Charlie

Word Practice

- Find 6 words.

- Choose the correct word for each sentence.

have	but	good

1. I ____________ a computer.

2. He is a ____________ person.

3. I'm sorry, ____________ I can't do it.

Sentence Practice

- Unscramble the sentences.

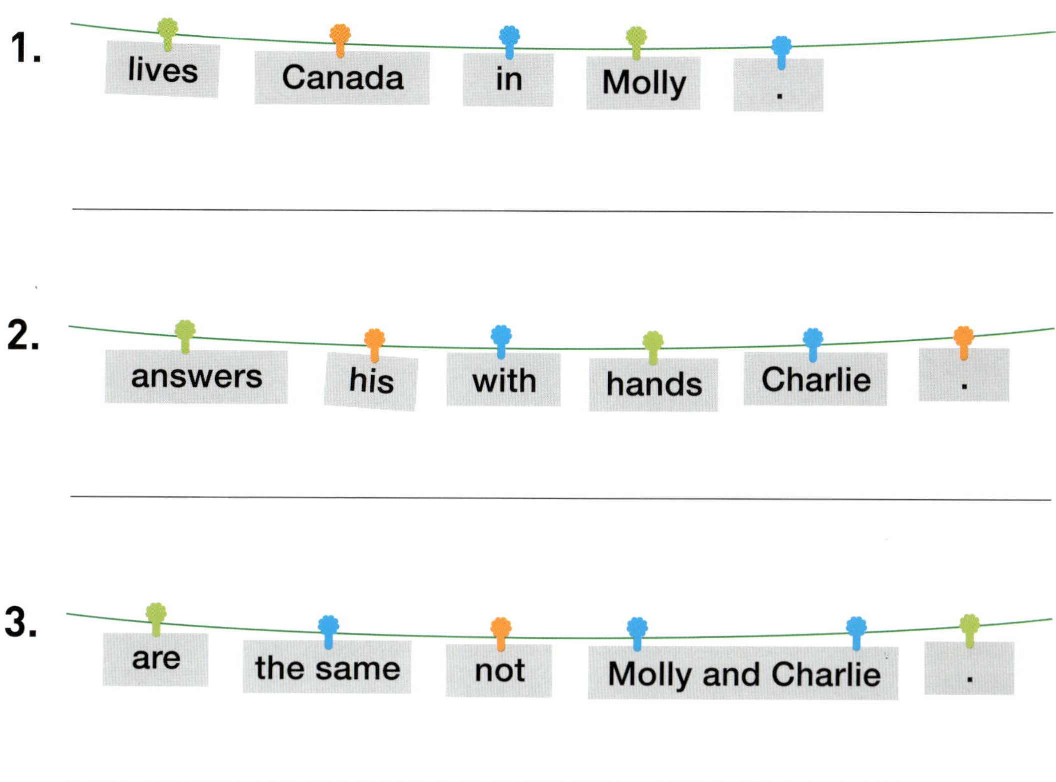

- Read the passage of the unit and match the sentence parts.

1. Molly has · · hear words.

2. Charlie can't · · a friend named Charlie.

3. She spells out · · words with her fingers.

4. Molly and Charlie are · · good friends.

04 Are You a Good Friend?

Word Practice

- Put the letters in the correct order. Then write the words.

1. p e h l

   ____

2. e h r e c

   ____

3. u n f

   ____

4. h a g l u

   ____

5. e f l e

   ____

6. d s a

   ____

- Choose the correct word for each sentence.

do	need	happy

1. Don't ____________ it.

2. I ____________ your help.

3. My parents are always ____________ .

Sentence Practice

- Unscramble the sentences.

1.

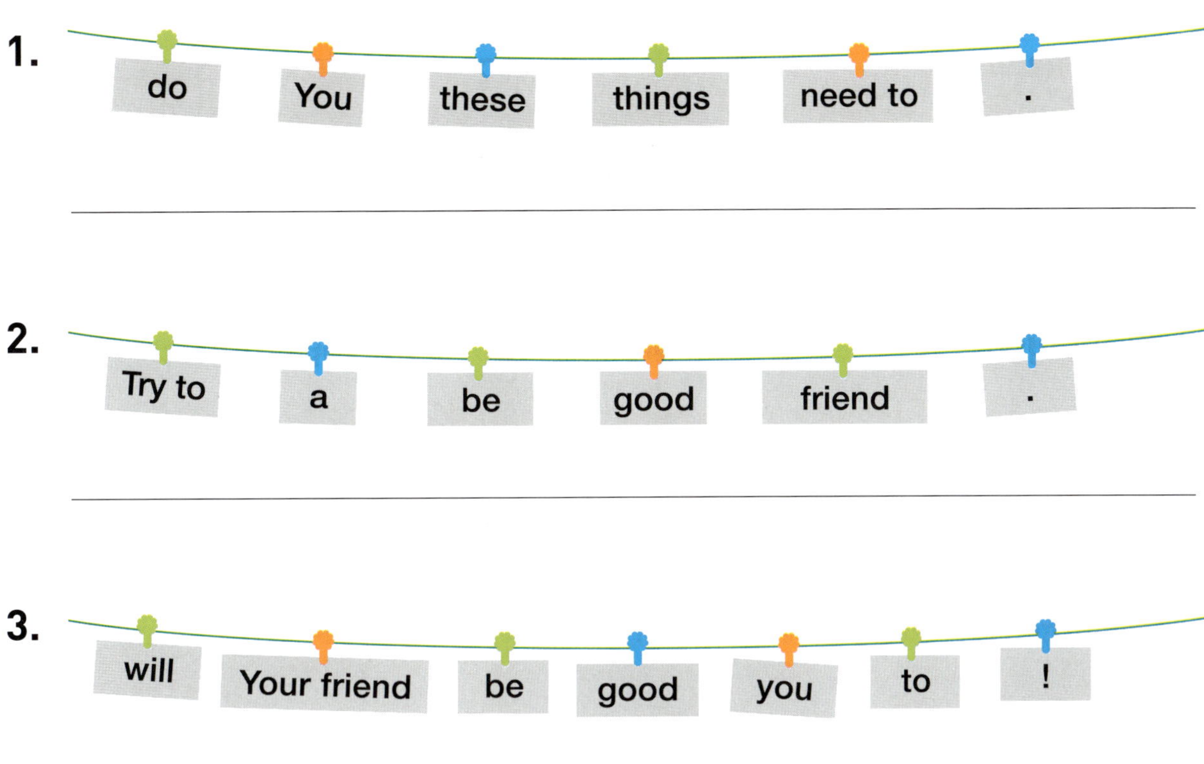

____

2.

____

3.

____

- Read the passage of the unit and match the sentence parts.

1. Have   •   • fun!

2. Help   •   • up your friend!

3. Cheer •   • with your friend!

4. Laugh •   • your friend!

01 Happy Birthday, Mom!

Word Practice

- Write the correct word for each picture. Then circle 6 words in the box.

1. _______________

2. _______________

3. _______________

4. _______________

5. _______________

6. _______________

t	r	v	p	o	c	r	a	i	f
l	i	v	i	n	g	r	o	o	m
e	b	i	r	t	h	d	a	y	k
q	t	d	o	r	s	s	e	r	d
d	k	i	k	k	x	k	y	k	e
a	o	t	r	i	k	s	p	j	o
a	v	v	w	o	e	d	j	h	h
h	t	u	e	g	v	b	k	i	e
w	s	m	e	d	o	a	y	g	c
e	u	w	o	d	m	j	f	s	s

- Choose the correct word for each sentence.

clap	suddenly	like

1. She talks _____________ a baby.

2. _____________ , he starts to run.

3. We _____________ our hands together.

Sentence Practice

- Unscramble the sentences.

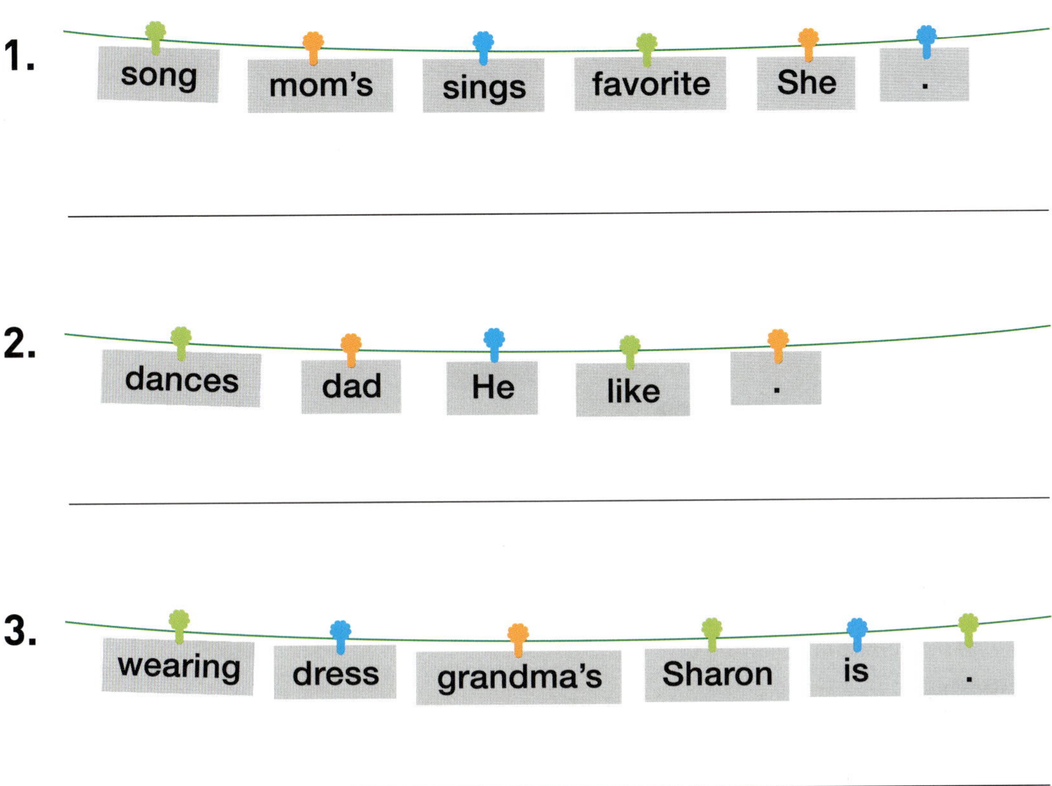

____

____

____

- Read the passage of the unit and match the sentence parts.

1. Today is   •   • in the living room.

2. Everyone is   •   • mom's birthday.

3. Suddenly,   •   • laughs.

4. Everyone   •   • Anna, Willy, and Sharon show up.

02 The Baseball Game

Word Practice

- Complete the crossword puzzle.

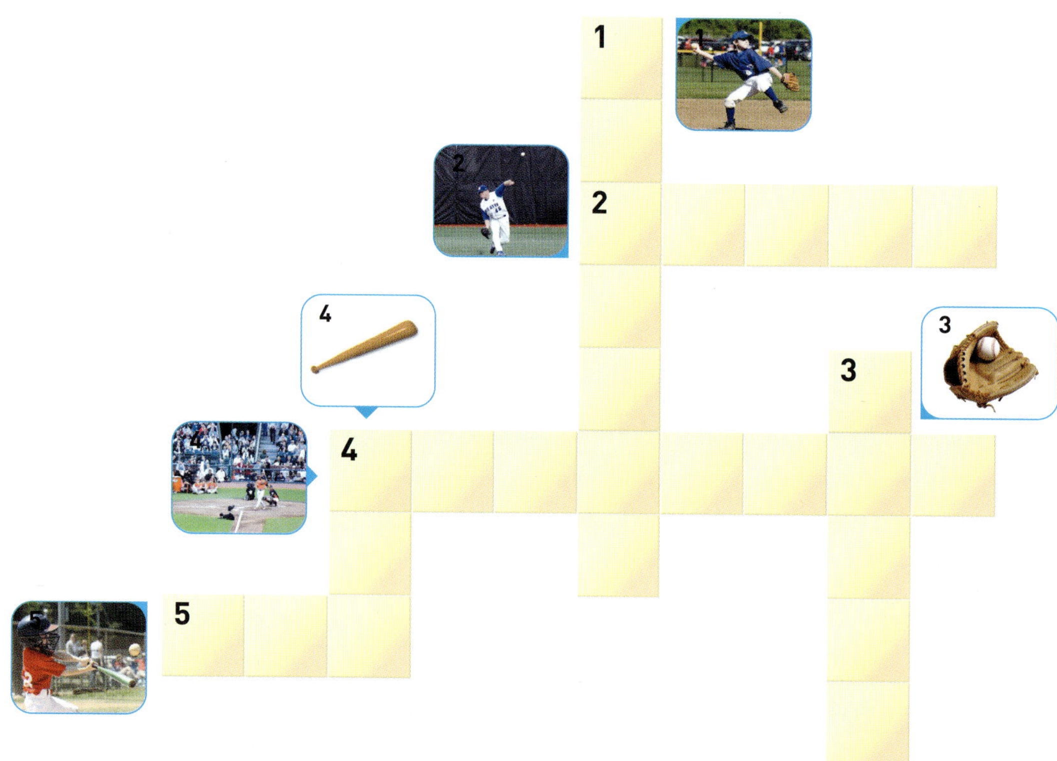

- Choose the correct word for each sentence.

> children   out   next

1. The _____________ swim in the pool.

2. You can come again _____________ time.

3. The players in our team are all _____________ .

Sentence Practice

- Unscramble the sentences.

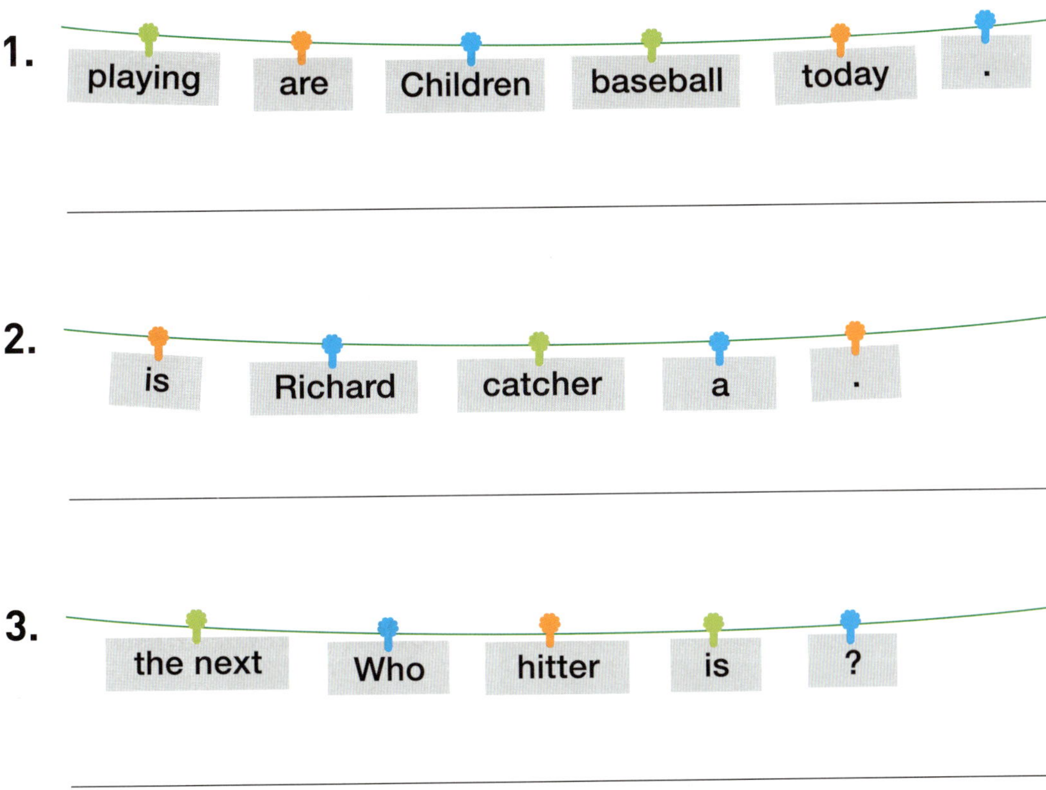

1. ____

2. ____

3. ____

- Read the passage of the unit and match the sentence parts.

1. Ben, Dennis, •   • and Richard are on the field.

2. Ben is •   • the ball with his bat.

3. Dennis hits •   • the ball with his glove.

4. Richard catches •   • a pitcher.

03 Manners at Classical Concerts

Word Practice

- Find 6 words.

- Choose the correct word for each sentence.

classical	start	bring

1. I like ______________ music.

2. Please, ______________ the camera!

3. The movie will ______________ soon.

Sentence Practice

- Unscramble the sentences.

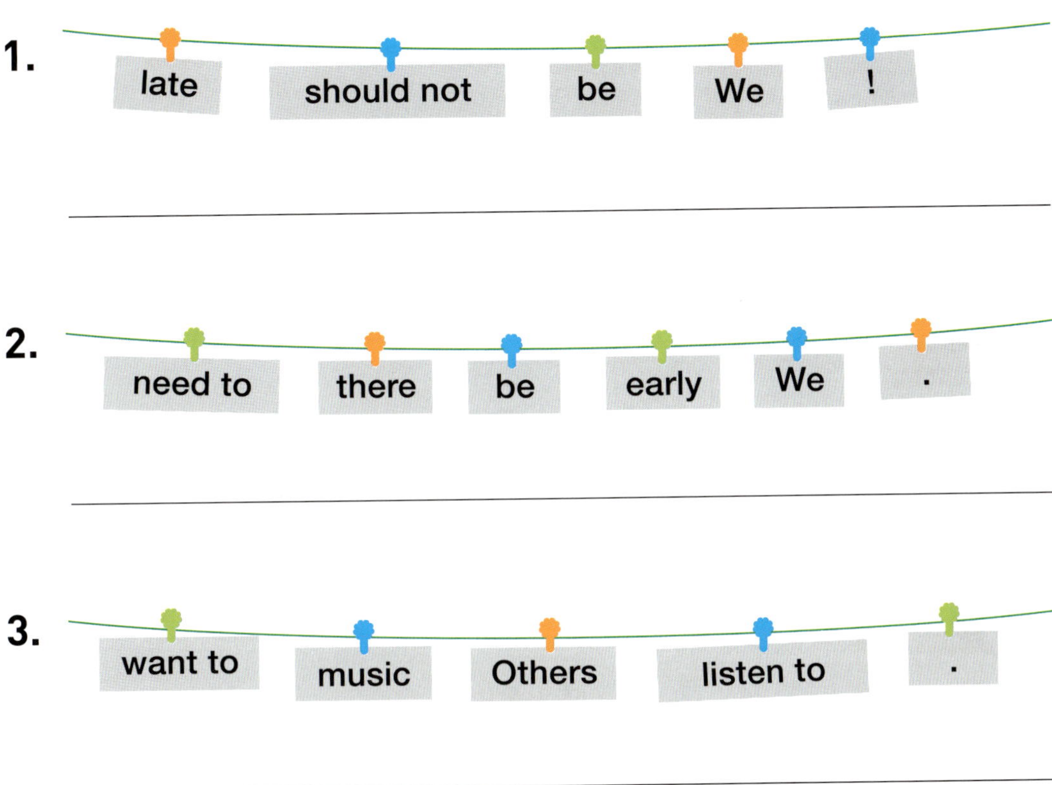

1. _______________________________________

2. _______________________________________

3. _______________________________________

- Read the passage of the unit and match the sentence parts.

1. Do you   •   • the doors close.

2. When the concert starts,   •   • like classical concerts?

3. We should   •   • take pictures!

4. We should not   •   • be quiet!

04 Folk Dancing

Word Practice

- Put the letters in the correct order. Then write the words.

1. u j m c s

____

2. a p l c

____

3. e s p t

____

4. f e t e

____

5. t m s p a

____

6. p s n i

____

- Choose the correct word for each sentence.

> lesson   beat   around

1. They dance to the ____________.

2. I want to take a piano ____________.

3. Children are circling ____________ the tree.

Sentence Practice

- Unscramble the sentences.

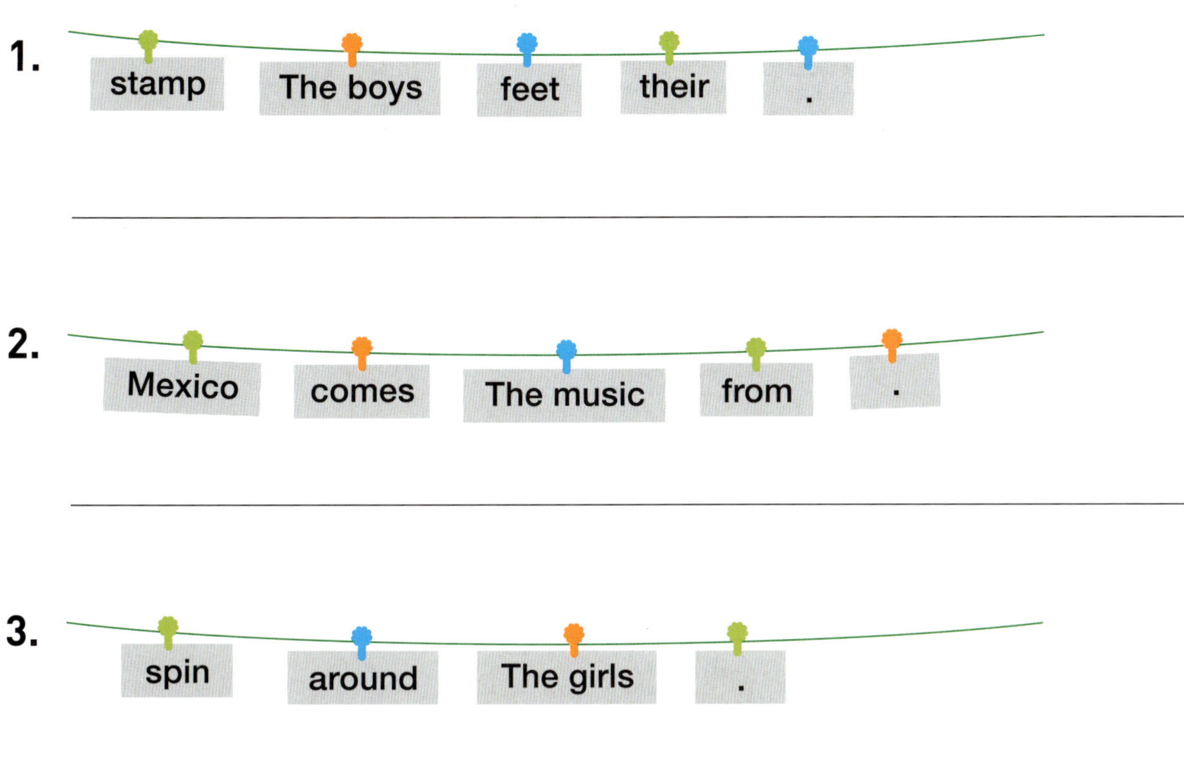

____

____

____

- Read the passage of the unit and match the sentence parts.

1. The children take   •   • to clap to the beat.

2. They learn   •   • folk dance lessons.

3. They dance   •   • fun for everyone.

4. Folk dancing is   •   • to a special kind of music.

01 Little Tomatoes

Word Practice

- Write the correct word for each picture. Then circle 6 words in the box.

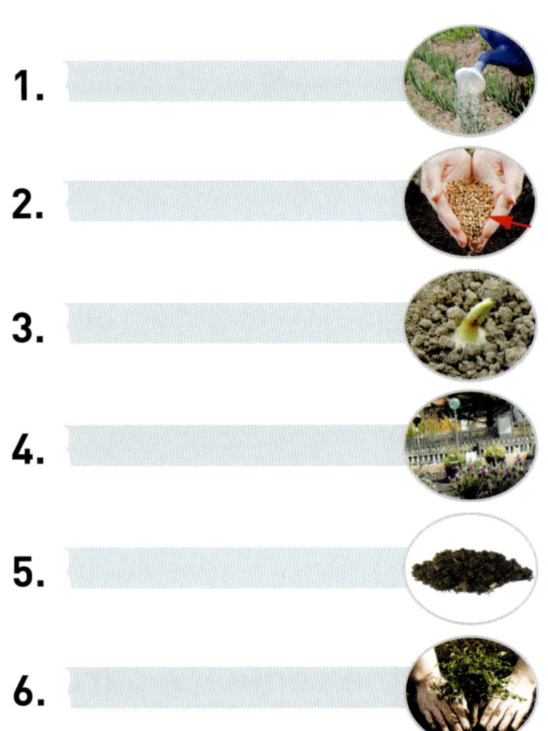

1. ___________

2. ___________

3. ___________

4. ___________

5. ___________

6. ___________

n	v	r	y	p	z	v	t
e	x	e	p	q	a	x	r
d	d	t	l	d	y	h	c
r	u	a	a	e	j	j	y
a	h	w	n	e	w	d	l
g	y	e	t	s	o	i	l
z	s	u	p	o	a	x	t
k	s	t	u	o	r	p	s

- Choose the correct word for each sentence.

tomato	later	worry

1. I'll call you ___________.

2. I love ___________ juice.

3. Don't ___________ and everything will be fine.

Sentence Practice

- Unscramble the sentences.

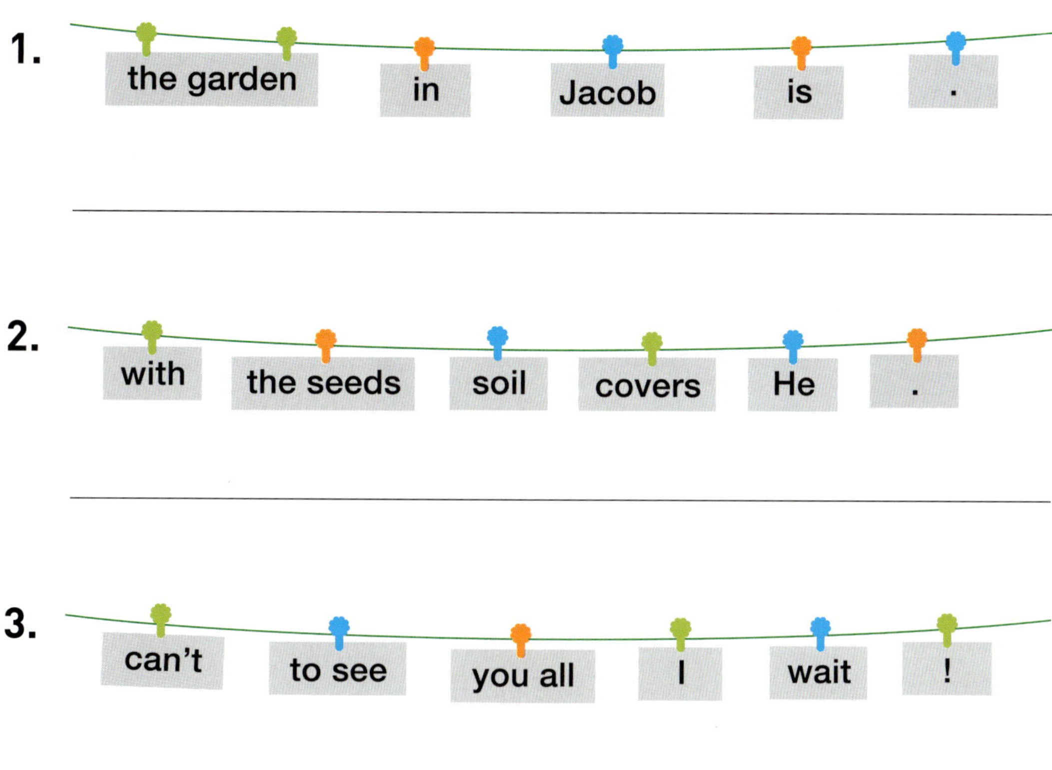

- Read the passage of the unit and match the sentence parts.

1. Jacob plants   •   • seeds in each hole.

2. He puts   •   • them every day.

3. He waters   •   • sees new sprouts.

4. The next day, he   •   • tomato seeds.

02 Yummy Apple!

Word Practice

- Complete the crossword puzzle.

- Choose the correct word for each sentence.

| high | reach | big |

1. He has a ____________ room.

2. My arm doesn't ____________ that window.

3. The plane is flying ____________ up in the sky.

Sentence Practice

- Unscramble the sentences.

1.

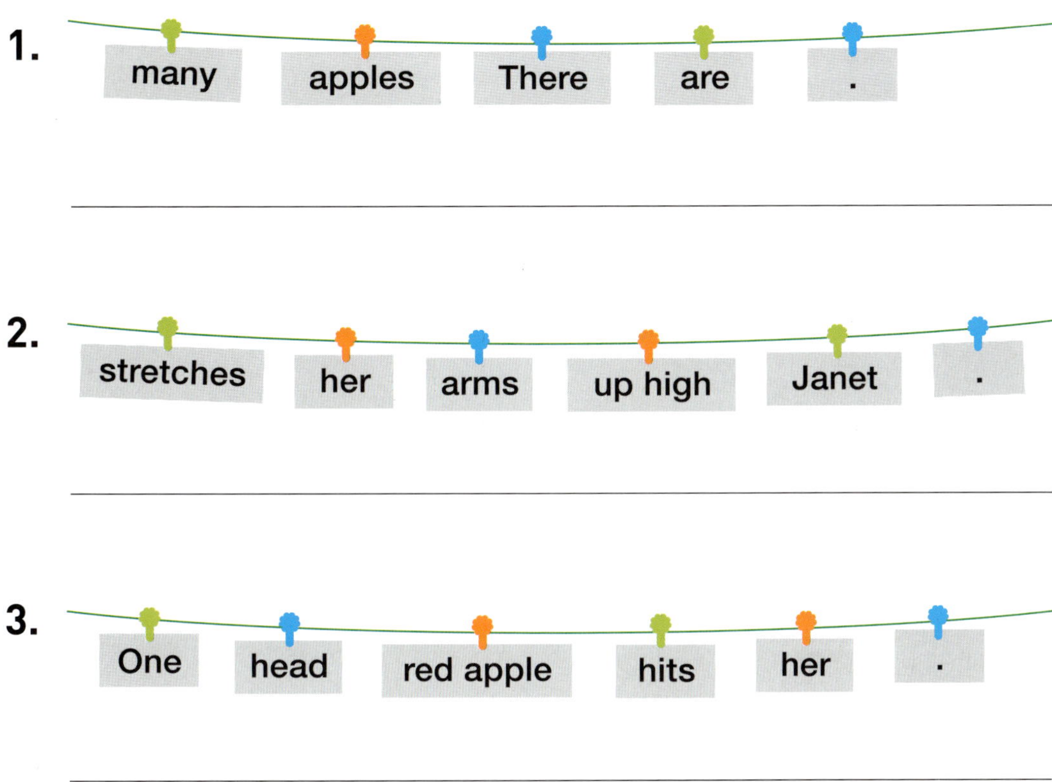

____

2.

____

3.

____

- Read the passage of the unit and match the sentence parts.

1. Janet cannot   •   •   blows.

2. Suddenly, the wind   •   •   on the ground.

3. The apple falls   •   •   reach the apples.

4. She picks up   •   •   the apple and takes a bite.

03 How Old is the Tree?

Word Practice

- Find 6 words.

- Choose the correct word for each sentence.

easy	find	count

1. Here's an ______________ question.

2. Can he ______________ the numbers?

3. How do you ______________ the answer?

Sentence Practice

- Unscramble the sentences.

1. 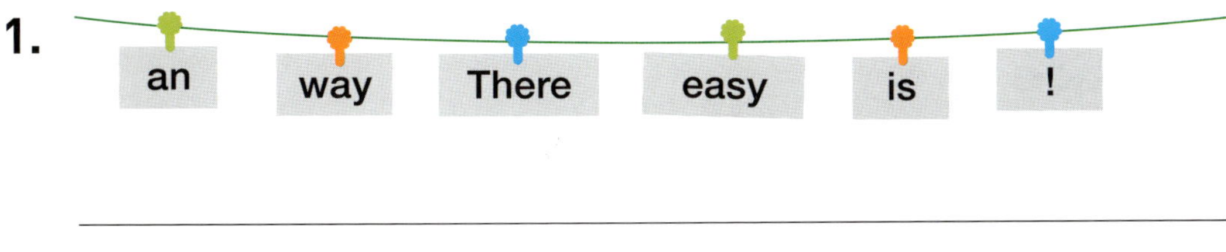

____

2. 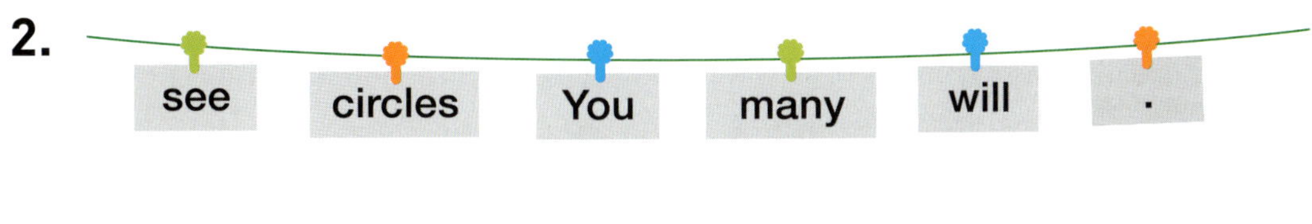

____

3. 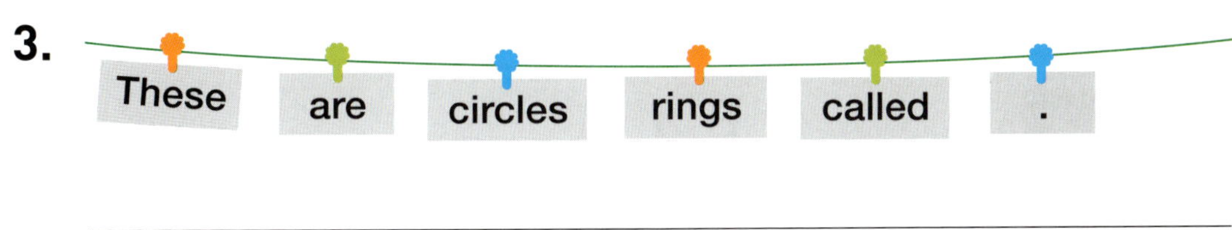

____

- Read the passage of the unit and match the sentence parts.

1. How do you   •   • find the age of a tree?

2. First, look at   •   • all the rings.

3. Second, count   •   • is a tree with 100 rings?

4. How old   •   • the trunk of a tree.

04 What are Some Parts of Plants?

Word Practice

- Put the letters in the correct order. Then write the words.

1. o r t o

   ____

2. i g l t h

   ____

3. l f w o r e

   ____

4. e l f a

   ____

5. t s m e

   ____

6. r i a

   ____

- Choose the correct word for each sentence.

part	carry	each

1. ______________ student has his own desk.

2. It can ______________ blood to the heart.

3. Your nose is a ______________ of your body.

Sentence Practice

- Unscramble the sentences.

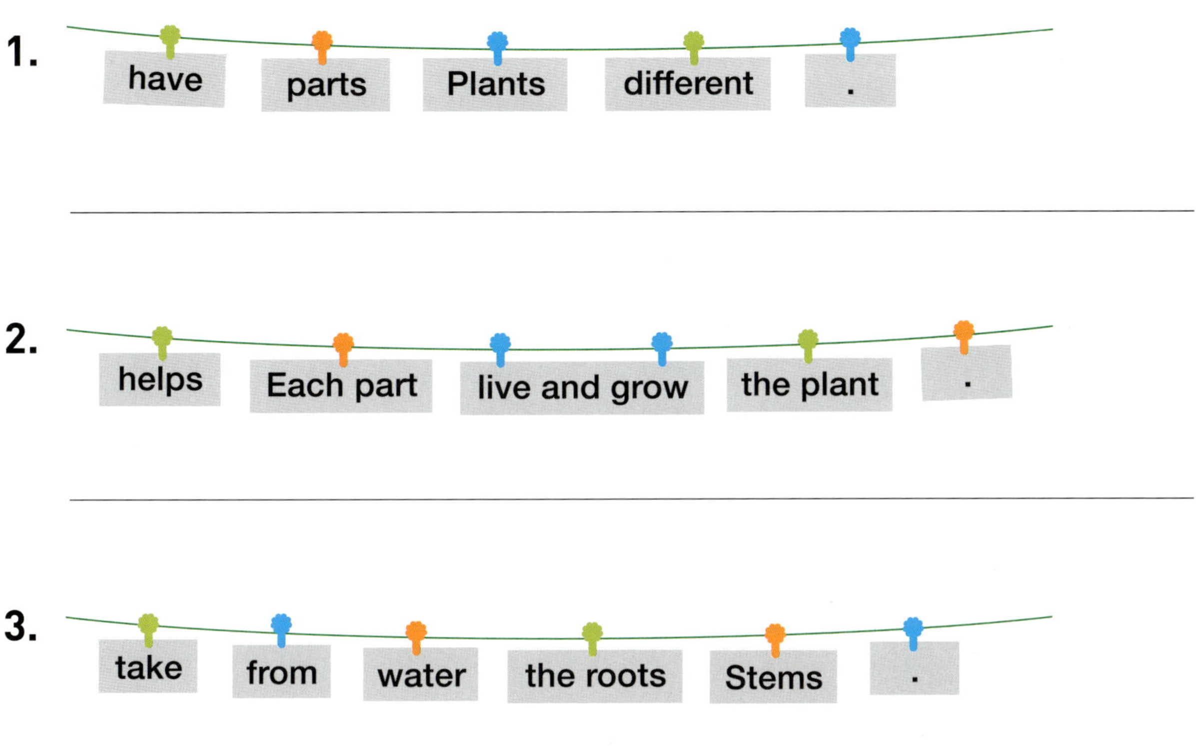

- Read the passage of the unit and match the sentence parts.

1. Roots hold   •   • water to other parts.

2. Stems carry   •   • the plant in the soil.

3. Leaves make   •   • seeds.

4. Flowers make   •   • food for the plant.

01 My Piggy Bank

Word Practice

- Write the correct word for each picture. Then circle 6 words in the box.

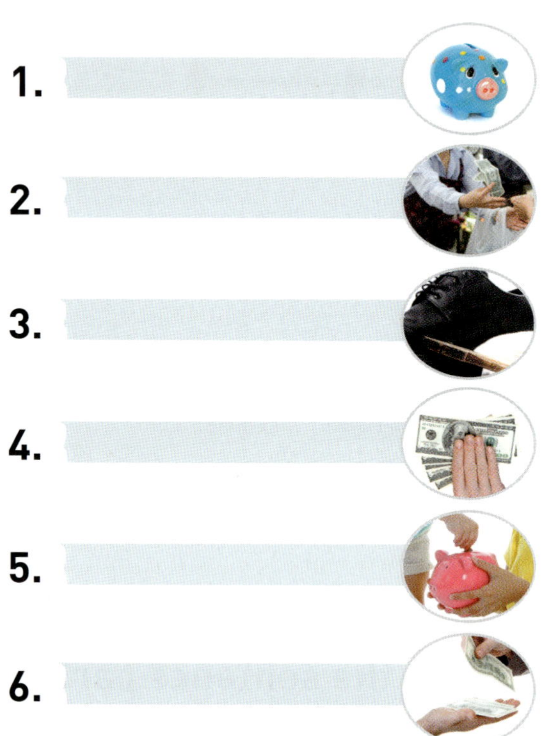

1. __________

2. __________

3. __________

4. __________

5. __________

6. __________

l	i	s	l	q	a	e	t	j	h
p	u	r	a	n	u	d	h	c	d
i	c	i	a	v	e	n	i	h	s
g	r	q	s	s	e	e	b	y	o
g	n	e	c	j	x	p	h	j	p
y	i	k	z	j	d	s	z	o	b
b	w	n	o	s	u	x	p	u	m
a	g	o	g	d	j	v	y	i	p
n	u	y	e	n	o	m	n	h	t
k	m	n	g	c	c	x	f	t	t

- Choose the correct word for each sentence.

shoes	put	will

1. I ____________ call you tonight.

2. The ____________ are under the table.

3. I ____________ my socks into the basket.

Sentence Practice

- Unscramble the sentences.

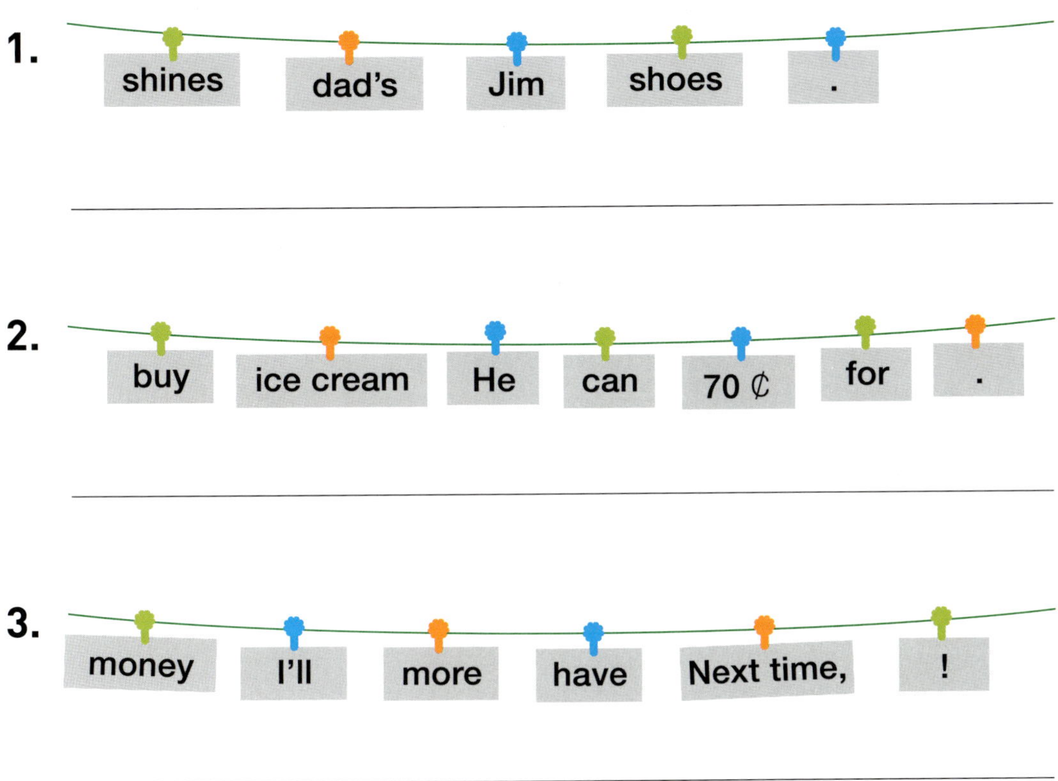

- Read the passage of the unit and match the sentence parts.

1. Jim can choose   •   •   chocolates for 50 ¢ .

2. He can buy   •   •   the money for later.

3. Or he can save   •   •   how to spend the money.

4. He puts   •   •   the money into the piggy bank.

02 My Busy Mom!

Word Practice

- Complete the crossword puzzle.

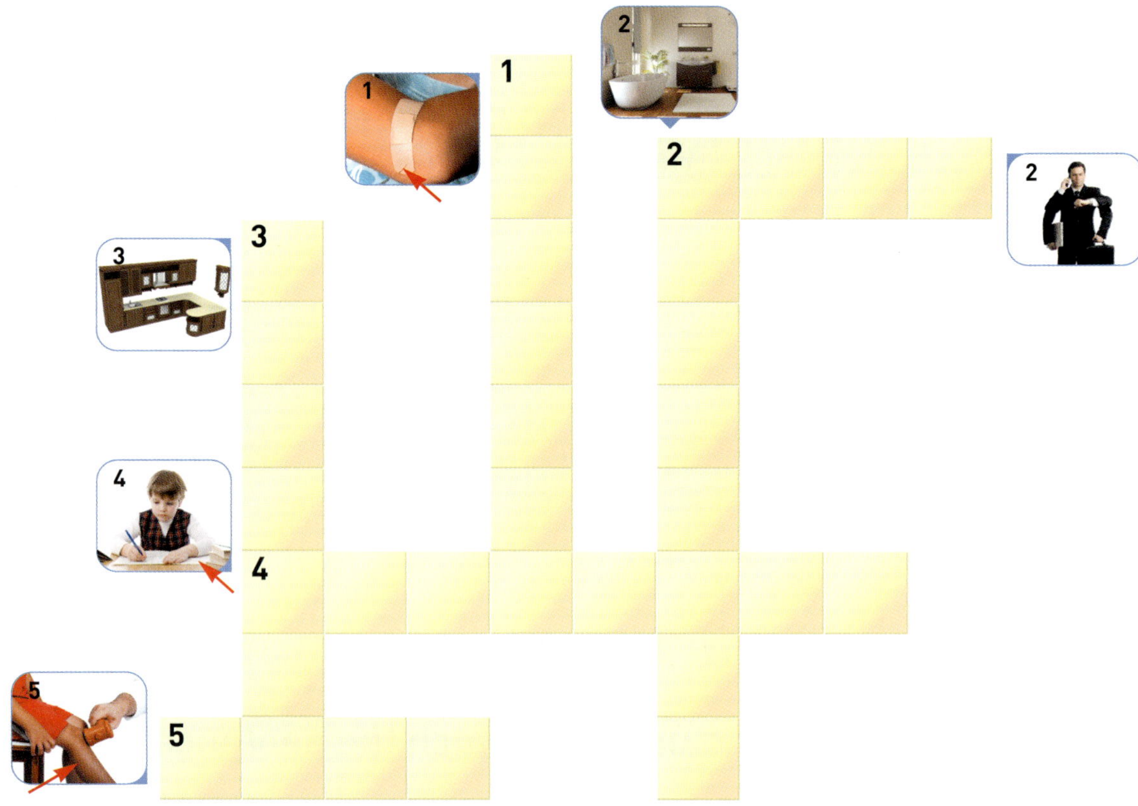

- Choose the correct word for each sentence.

> knock   dining room   brother

1. He is in the _______________ .

2. I am sitting next to my _______________ .

3. We hear a _______________ on the door.

Sentence Practice

- Unscramble the sentences.

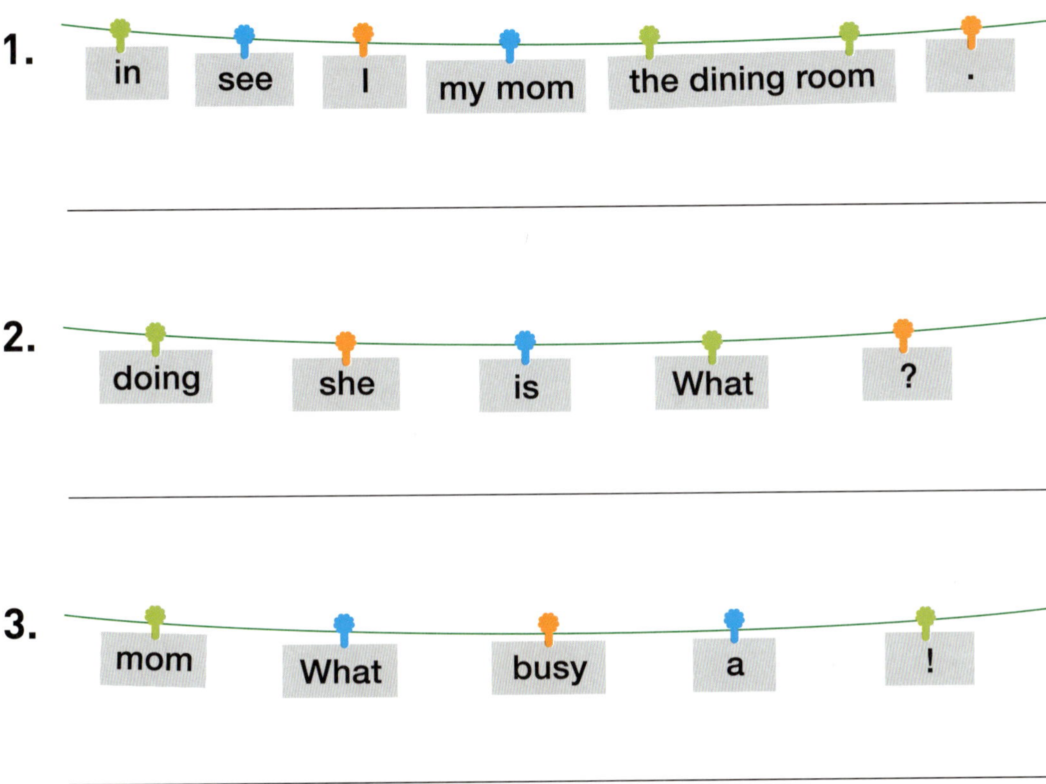

- Read the passage of the unit and match the sentence parts.

1. What is •   • my brother with his homework.

2. She is cooking •   • in the kitchen.

3. She is helping •   • she doing?

4. She is putting •   • a bandage on my sister's knee.

03 Interview with a Farmer

Word Practice

- Find 6 words.

- Choose the correct word for each sentence.

take	send	store

1. It may ______________ a lot of time.

2. I'll ______________ you a card tomorrow.

3. The ______________ opens at nine o'clock.

Sentence Practice

- Unscramble the sentences.

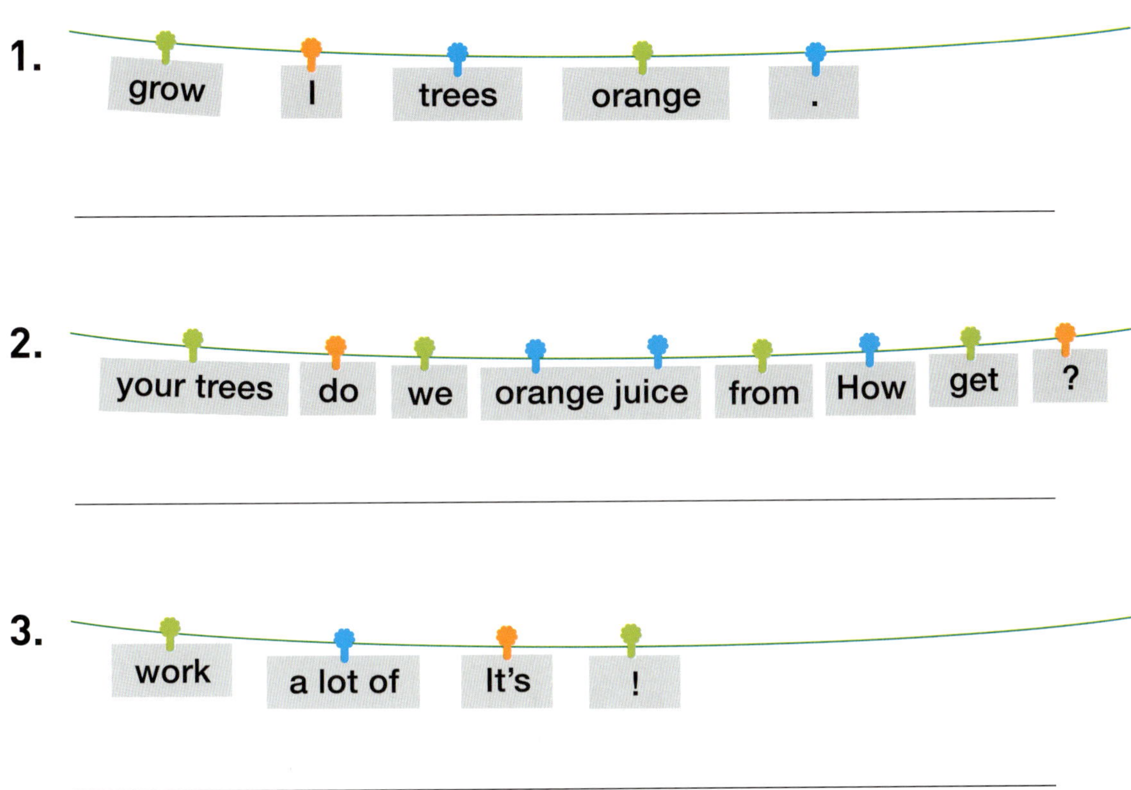

- Read the passage of the unit and match the sentence parts.

1. We pick   •   • the oranges.

2. We move them   •   • to the squeezing machine.

3. We put the juice   •   • are sent to the stores.

4. The juice containers •   • into containers.

04 Why do People Work?

Word Practice

- Put the letters in the correct order. Then write the words.

1. e h n e e l p o t

2. y p a

3. o s g o d

4. o b j

5. l c r e k

6. a n r e

- Choose the correct word for each sentence.

outside	service	why

1. It is raining ______________.

2. ______________ do you ask?

3. The ______________ in the restaurant is not good.

Sentence Practice

- Unscramble the sentences.

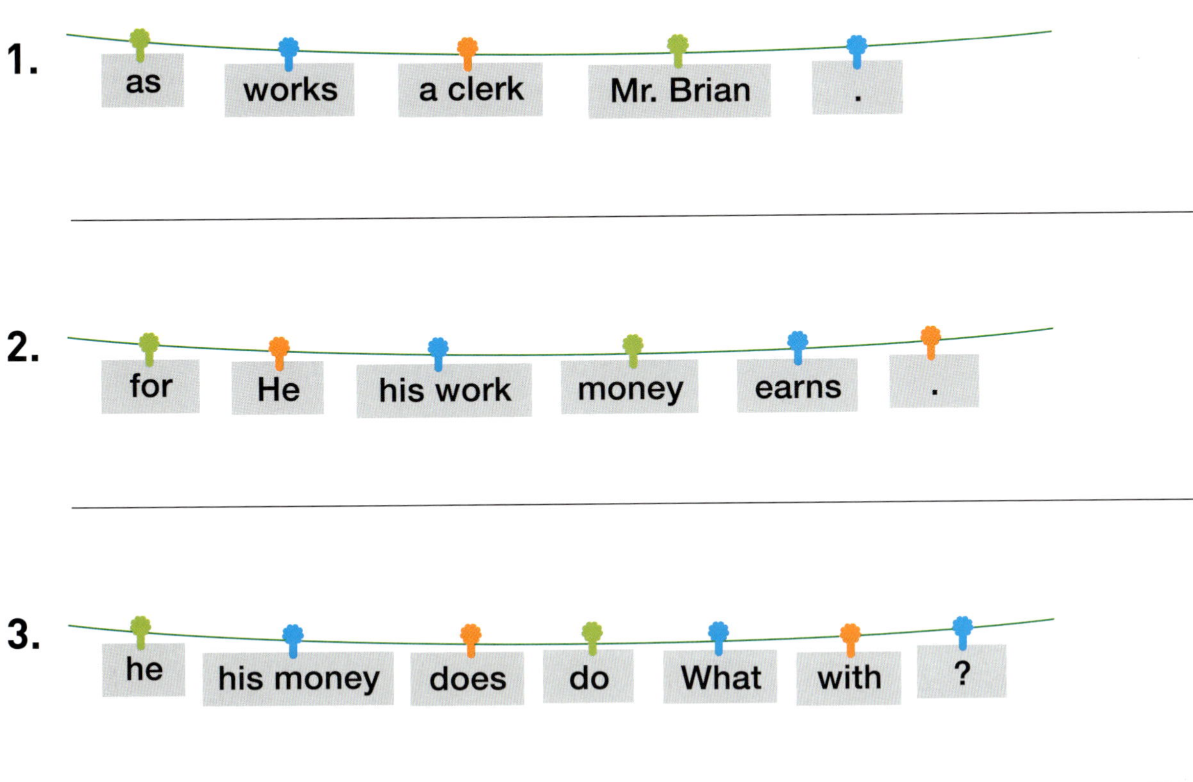

- Read the passage of the unit and match the sentence parts.

1. Most people   •   • people work?

2. Why do   •   • goods like food and clothes.

3. They work   •   • to get goods and services.

4. They buy   •   • have jobs.

01 Mother Nature's Holidays

Word Practice

- Write the correct word for each picture. Then circle 6 words in the box.

1. ___________
2. ___________
3. ___________
4. ___________
5. ___________
6. ___________

```
p  w  i  n  t  e  r  e
e  n  p  j  d  s  s  k
e  d  q  y  w  k  v  a
l  s  y  v  z  y  b  w
s  p  r  i  n  g  i  z
m  a  n  f  w  o  r  j
g  s  b  p  d  w  d  r
s  b  t  k  z  p  d  y
```

- Choose the correct word for each sentence.

hard	during	break

1. We study ___________ every day.

2. He needed a ___________ from his work.

3. What do you do ___________ the weekend?

Sentence Practice

- Unscramble the sentences.

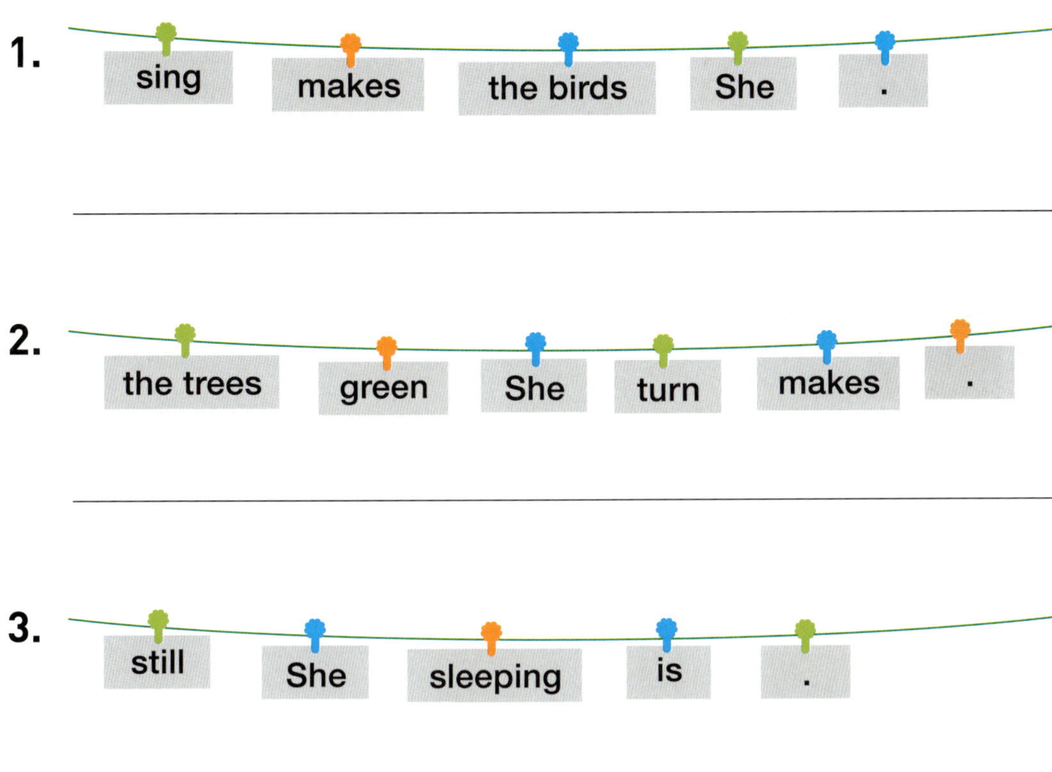

- Read the passage of the unit and match the sentence parts.

1. Mother Nature is   •   • has come.

2. During winter, she   •   • takes a long break.

3. The spring   •   • busy every spring.

4. Wake   •   • up! Mother Nature!

02 Spring Rain

Word Practice

- Complete the crossword puzzle.

- Choose the correct word for each sentence.

sound	cotton	blow

1. The flags ____________ in the wind.

2. The phone makes a strange ____________ .

3. Two girls are eating ____________ candies.

Sentence Practice

- **Unscramble the sentences.**

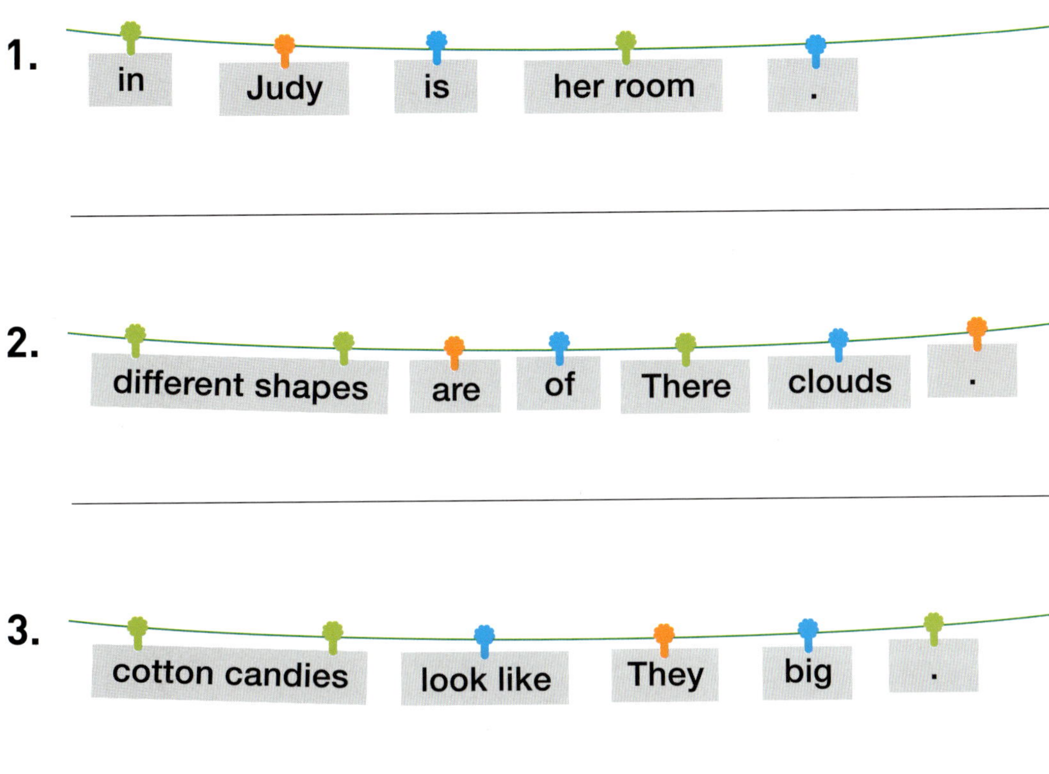

____

____

____

- **Read the passage of the unit and match the sentence parts.**

1. She hears   •   • hitting the window.

2. Rain is   •   • blows in her face.

3. Some fresh air •   • the warm air.

4. She feels   •   • some tapping sounds.

03 Clothes and Activities for the Season

Word Practice

- Find 6 words.

- Choose the correct word for each sentence.

season	coat	ski

1. Do you know how to ____________?

2. Spring is my favorite ____________.

3. She is wearing a fur ____________.

Sentence Practice

- Unscramble the sentences.

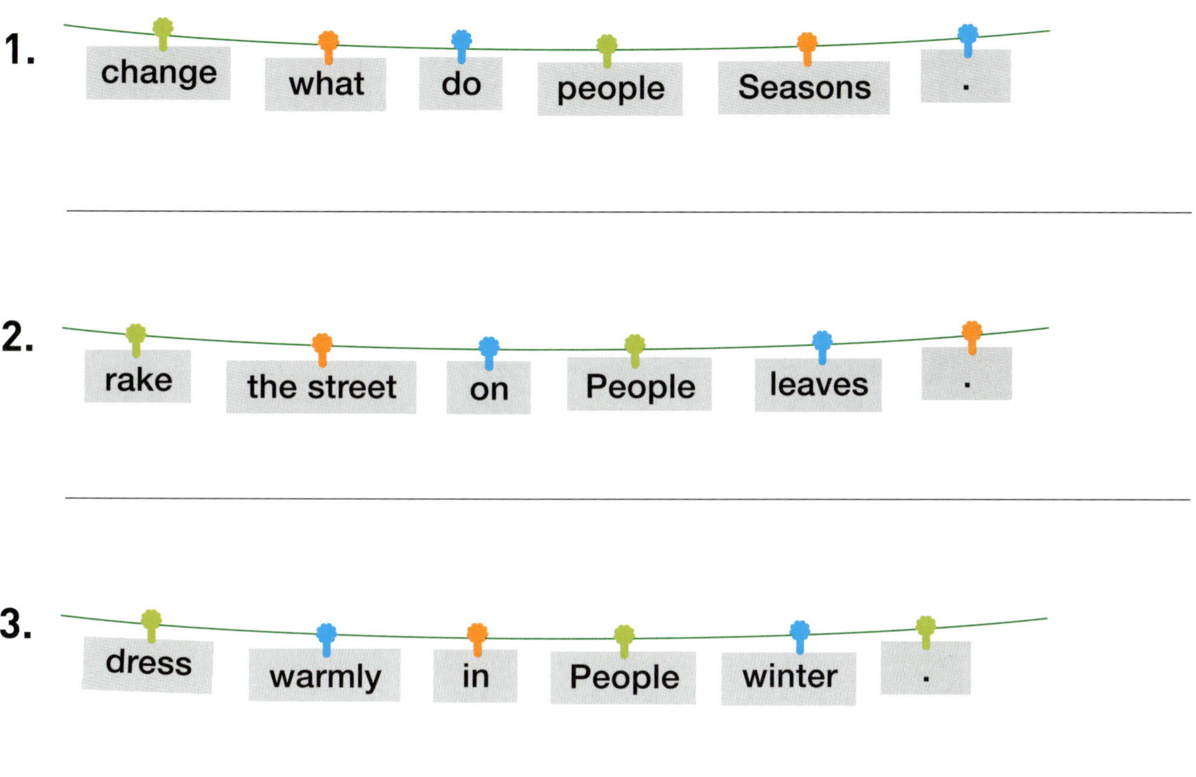

- Read the passage of the unit and match the sentence parts.

1. Seasons change • • what people wear.

2. In spring, people • • wear light jackets.

3. In autumn, people • • wear long pants and sweaters.

4. People wear • • coats and boots in winter.

04 Saving Water

Word Practice

- **Put the letters in the correct order. Then write the words.**

1. i d k r n

   ____

2. u f t c a e

   ____

3. o k c o

   ____

4. h r s e w o

   ____

5. t e r a h

   ____

6. s u l f h

   ____

- **Choose the correct word(s) for each sentence.**

enough	turn off	often

1. Please _______________ the TV.

2. He _______________ writes to his friends.

3. We don't have _______________ chairs in the classroom.

Sentence Practice

- Unscramble the sentences.

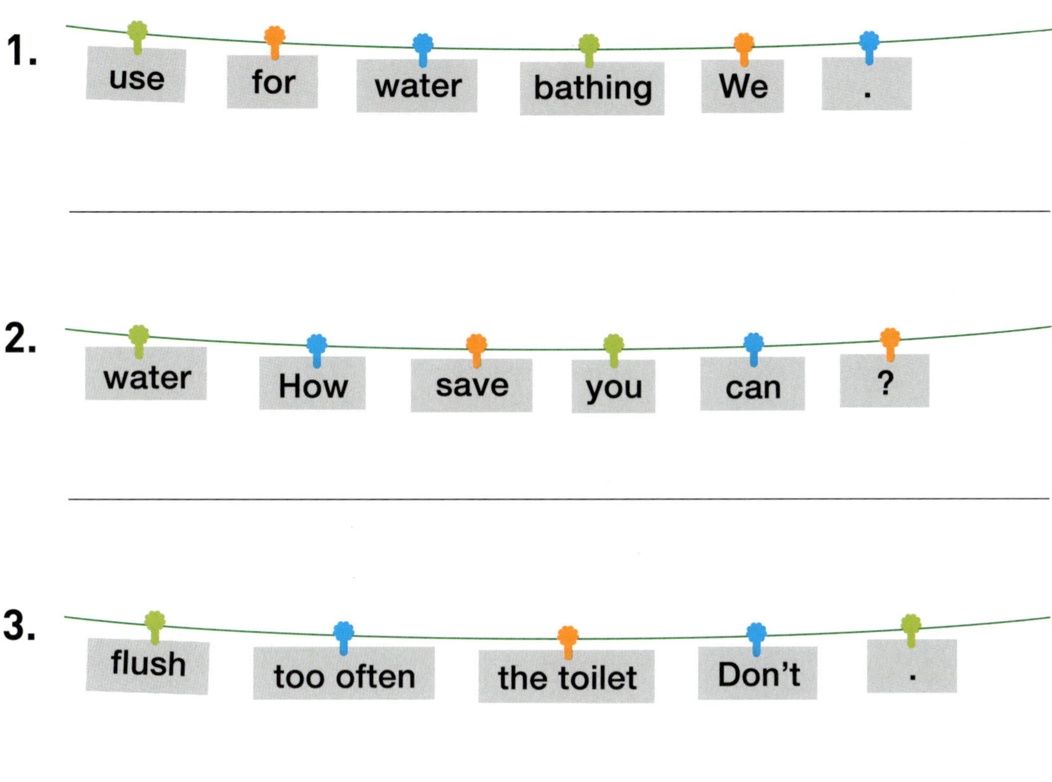

____

____

____

- Read the passage of the unit and match the sentence parts.

1. We need   •   • enough water on earth.

2. We don't have   •   • when brushing your teeth.

3. Turn off the faucet   •   • water to live.

4. We need to work   •   • together to save water.

MEMO

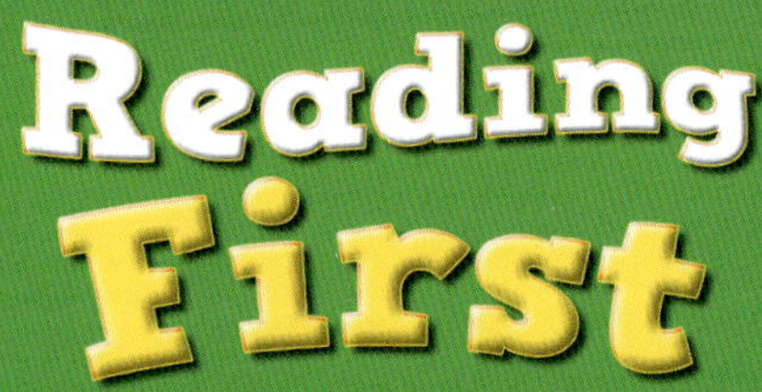

Reading First

Reading First is a three-leveled reading series designed for beginner students to strengthen the foundation of reading comprehension skills. Accompanied by fascinating visuals, this series equips students with a wide vocabulary while developing reading comprehension skills. Themes based on current North American curriculum guide students to use their imagination as they explore various fiction stories and nonfiction articles. The follow-on activities are designed to strengthen their speaking and writing skills. This series is full of all the necessary tools students need to improve their overall English ability.

Key Features:
★ Background knowledge and pre-reading vocabulary activities
★ Captivating images to stimulate imaginations
★ Theme-based topics with 2 fiction stories and 2 nonfiction articles
★ Basic reading comprehension skills presented with easy visual formats
★ Variation in vocabulary expansion activities
★ Further speaking and writing activities
★ Full engagement in reading with lively animated MP3 files
★ Workbook for word practice and sentence practice

Components
★ Student Book / Workbook
★ MP3 Files / Answer Keys
Download resources at **www.wcbooks.co.kr**

Reading First Series

WorldCom Edu   www.wcbooks.co.kr